Equity Derivatives Explained

Mohamed Bouzoubaa

palgrave
macmillan

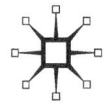

© Mohamed Bouzoubaa 2014

All rights reserved. No reproduction, copy or transmission of this publication may be made without written permission.

No portion of this publication may be reproduced, copied or transmitted save with written permission or in accordance with the provisions of the Copyright, Designs and Patents Act 1988, or under the terms of any licence permitting limited copying issued by the Copyright Licensing Agency, Saffron House, 6–10 Kirby Street, London EC1N 8TS.

Any person who does any unauthorized act in relation to this publication may be liable to criminal prosecution and civil claims for damages.

The author has asserted his right to be identified as the author of this work in accordance with the Copyright, Designs and Patents Act 1988.

First published 2014 by
PALGRAVE MACMILLAN

Palgrave Macmillan in the UK is an imprint of Macmillan Publishers Limited, registered in England, company number 785998, of Houndmills, Basingstoke, Hampshire RG21 6XS.

Palgrave Macmillan in the US is a division of St Martin's Press LLC, 175 Fifth Avenue, New York, NY 10010.

Palgrave Macmillan is the global academic imprint of the above companies and has companies and representatives throughout the world.

Palgrave® and Macmillan® are registered trademarks in the United States, the United Kingdom, Europe and other countries

ISBN: 978–1–137–33553–1

This book is printed on paper suitable for recycling and made from fully managed and sustained forest sources. Logging, pulping and manufacturing processes are expected to conform to the environmental regulations of the country of origin.

A catalogue record for this book is available from the British Library.

A catalog record for this book is available from the Library of Congress.

To my parents and family
And special thanks to Lamia

Contents

List of Figures ix

1 Fundamentals 1
   1.1 Stock Markets and Indices 1
   1.2 Interest Rates and Dividends 2
   1.3 Short Selling and Borrowing 8
   1.4 Volatility Concepts 10

2 Inside the World of Equity Derivatives 14
   2.1 The Sell Side 14
   2.2 The Buy Side 19

3 Forwards, Futures and Swaps 22
   3.1 Futures Markets 22
   3.2 Forward Contracts 26
   3.3 Equity Swaps 29
   3.4 Dividend Swaps 35

4 Pricing Vanilla Options 38
   4.1 European Calls and Puts 38
   4.2 Hedging Cost Principle 43
   4.3 Pricing Vanillas 45
   4.4 American Options 49
   4.5 Asian Options 52

5 Risk Management Tools 54
   5.1 All About the Greeks 54
   5.2 Greeks Closed Relationships 68
   5.3 Choosing the Right Model 71

6 Strategies Built around Vanillas 73
   6.1 Equity Hedging the Traditional Way 73
   6.2 Vertical Spreads 77
   6.3 Bear Put Spread 79
   6.4 Collars and Three-Ways 81
   6.5 Butterfly and Condor Spreads 83
   6.6 Straddles and Strangles 86

7 Yield Enhancement Solutions   89
   7.1 Equity Structured Notes   89
   7.2 Playing with Volatility   91
   7.3 Equity Dispersion Derivatives   93
   7.4 Dynamic Indices   94

Index   97

List of Figures

1.1:	AUD denominated upward-sloping yield curve	5
1.2:	Downward-sloping curve	5
1.3:	Humped yield curve	5
1.4:	Short selling scheme	8
1.5:	Implied volatility skew versus flat volatility graph	12
1.6:	Term structure of volatility	13
2.1:	Communication scheme between the sell side front office and the buy side when a reverse enquiry takes place	18
3.1:	Margin call mechanism	24
3.2:	Terms of a one-year forward contract	26
3.3:	Payoff patterns from long and short forward positions	27
3.4:	Cash flows exchanged in a three-month bullet equity swap	30
3.5:	Financing and execution of the purchase of shares by a bank on behalf of the client	33
3.6:	Exchanged cash flows during the life of a swap	33
3.7:	Outcomes of an equity swap	34
3.8:	Diagram of an equity swap transaction	35
3.9:	Dividend swaps mechanism	37
4.1:	Moneyness of European call and put options	39
4.2:	Payoff of a long ATM call position and payoff of a short OTM call position	39
4.3:	Comparison of profits from long positions in a European call and a forward contract with identical strikes at 110%	40
4.4:	Payoff of a long position in a European put with strike at 100% and from a short position in a European put with strike at 110%	41
4.5:	Comparison of profits from long positions in a European put and a forward contract with identical strikes	42
4.6:	Terms of a two-year European put option	43
4.7:	Log-normal distribution	45

4.8:	Cumulative probability up to the standardized normal value	46
4.9:	Price of a one-year European call struck at 100% with respect to the underlying spot price	47
4.10:	Price of a one-year European put with strike at 100% with respect to the underlying spot price	47
5.1:	Price of a forward contract with respect to the underlying stock's price	55
5.2:	Impact of time on the delta of a European call	56
5.3:	Effects of volatility on the delta of a European call	57
5.4:	Delta of a European put option with respect to the underlying stock's price for different maturities	58
5.5:	Gamma of a European option with respect to the underlying stock's price for different maturities	61
5.6:	Vega of a European put option with respect to the underlying stock's price for different maturities	63
5.7:	Theta of a European call option with respect to the underlying stock's price for different maturities	65
5.8:	Theta of a European put option with respect to the underlying stock's price for different maturities	65
5.9:	Rho of a European call option with respect to the underlying stock's price for different maturities	67
5.10:	Rho of a European put option with respect to the underlying stock's price for different maturities	67
6.1:	Profit graph from a short covered call position	74
6.2:	Profit graph associated with a protective put strategy	76
6.3:	Payoff and profit of a call spread strategy	78
6.4:	Bearish put spread versus vanilla put	80
6.5:	Profit at maturity from an equity collar composed of a long position in the underlying stock and a zero-cost short risk-reversal position with strikes at 80% and 120%.	82
6.6:	Profit at maturity from adding a three-way with strikes at 60%/80%/130% to a stock portfolio	83
6.7:	Payoff and profit of a short butterfly spread strategy	84
6.8:	Payoff and profit of a short condor spread strategy	85
6.9:	Payoff and profit of a long straddle strategy	87
6.10:	Payoff and profit of a long strangle strategy	88
7.1:	Composition and payoff of a three-year equity structure note based on S&P 500 index	90

1 Fundamentals

1.1 Stock Markets and Indices

The most traditional way for companies to raise funds and invest them in profitable new projects is through the introduction of shares in the primary market. Stock exchanges are used as channels to sell shares of ownership of the company through Initial Public Offerings (IPOs); these shares can then be exchanged and traded in secondary markets. Liquidity is an important parameter of stock exchanges as it enables market participants to quickly and easily buy and sell the equity instruments they invest in.

Stocks are listed in exchange-traded (also called "listed") markets; but equity derivatives can be traded in not just those markets but also in over-the-counter (OTC) markets. Here, we discuss the main features and particularities of these two markets. Exchange-traded markets are organized and regulated, and only standardized financial contracts are listed; on a stock to be traded there can be only a fixed list of options, with predetermined strikes and maturities.

If an investor would like to buy a call option with a very specific strike and target maturity date, they might not find one with those particular features listed on exchange-traded markets. Therefore, they would need to buy it through an OTC market. In these markets, participants trade directly with each other and enter into customized financial transactions; the contracts are designed and issued by financial institutions to make a perfect fit for the needs of investors.

To draw an analogy showing the difference between products traded on an exchange-traded market and an OTC market: If you decide to buy a shirt from a shop, you will only find a range of standardized colors, sizes and styles; this is similar to trading in listed markets. But if you have a very clear idea about the type and style of shirt you want to buy, and you decide to tailor-make it to suit you, that is similar to trading in OTC markets.

Apart from the structural features of the listed and OTC markets, there is a very important difference with regard to the nature of risk between these two markets. Bear in mind that OTC markets are less regulated and exhibit more credit and counterparty risk for investors than listed markets. This is mainly due to the fact that OTC market participants directly face each other through less standardized contracts; this chapter will give a more detailed explanation of the concepts of credit and counterparty risks. Also, most of the sophisticated and complex equity derivatives are traded in OTC markets.

As its name implies, a stock index can be viewed as a formula that provides a representative market return. The most commonly used weighting schemes for stock indices are *price-weighted*, *value-weighted* and *float-weighted*. Here, we briefly discuss their main characteristics and differences as well as their advantages and drawbacks.

A *price-weighted* index is defined as the arithmetical average of the prices of its underlying stocks. The main advantage of such an index is that it is easy to compute, and there are several other advantages: it can also provide a longer performance record, as a database of historical prices is more widely available, and it can expose several biases such as the greater impact of higher-priced stocks on the index value. However, a price-weighted index implicitly assumes that an investor will hold one share of each stock in the index; but in practice it is rare for investors to follow such a strategy. The Nikkei 225 and Dow Jones Industrial Average are both examples of price-weighted stock market indexes.

A *value-weighted* index, also called "market capitalization-weighted" index, is computed by summing the total market value of all the underlying stocks composing the index. Each total market value is calculated as the current stock price times the number of shares outstanding. This index weighting scheme assumes that an investor holds each company in the index according to its relative market value weight. Value-weighted indices are better representatives of changes in aggregate wealth. However, the primary bias of value-weighted indices is that firms with higher market capitalization have a greater impact on the index. France's CAC 40 index is an example of market value-weighted indices.

The S&P 500 index also used to be calculated as a value-weighted index, but has been changed to a *float-adjusted weighting*. A free float-adjusted market capitalization index can be considered as a subtype of a value-weighted index, as the only difference in the calculation method is replacing the number of outstanding shares with the number of shares that are actually available for trading. The "free-float problem" refers to the fact that many firms have shares that are closely held or not available for public trading. Only firms' freely traded shares should be included in float-weighted indices.

The float-adjusted index is considered by many market participants as the best weighting scheme, as it assumes that investors hold all the publically available shares of each company in the index. Therefore, it is considered more representative of the market and can be more easily tracked.

Stock indices are not initially intended as a trading vehicle, that is, one cannot buy or sell an index *per se*. If an investor wishes to gain exposure to a specific market, they can realize a "beta" exposure by investing in tradable instruments designed to replicate this index. (Without entering into too much detail, as this is not the main subject of this handbook, beta exposures can be realized by using index mutual funds, closed-end funds, exchange-traded funds or derivatives.)

1.2 Interest Rates and Dividends

Interest can be defined as a premium paid by a borrower to a lender in compensation for the lender deferring the use of their funds by lending them to the borrower. The interest rate agreed depends on the terms and conditions of the contract signed between borrower and lender. Indeed, the borrowing/lending contract can be a loan, a mortgage, a bond or a more sophisticated contract. The interest rate agreed will depend on the specifications of this contract as well as the creditworthiness of the counterparty, that is the borrower.

Whenever one party lends money to a borrower, the lender bears a credit risk, that is the risk that the borrower will not, whether willingly or unwillingly, fulfill their future obligations under the borrowing/lending contract; the lender is subject to the risk of not getting the agreed future interest or/and principal cash flows. The higher the credit risk borne by the lender, the higher the interest rate.

Credit ratings are used to give an indication of the ability of an entity to meet its current and future obligations under a specified financial transaction. Credit rating agencies such as Standard & Poor's, Moody's Investors Service and Fitch Group use the financial history of a company combined with its balance sheet to assess its credit rating. These ratings are then used by a lender to price the interest rate they offer whenever credit risk arises in a transaction with a specific counterparty.

The different types of credit risk include *default risk, credit spread risk* and *downgrade risk*. Without going into detail, it may be of interest to know that there are many methods for managing credit risk, including Value at Risk (VaR), limiting exposure to any single debtor, marking to market, using payment netting arrangements, using credit derivatives, setting credit standards, and assigning collateral to loans.

Interest rates are usually expressed as a percentage of the principal for a period of one year. For any given currency, the interest rate will decrease as trustworthiness of the borrower counterparty increases and terms that help control the credit risk are agreed on. In other words, the higher the risk of lending, the higher the cost of borrowing.

Let's take the case of Metal Limited, a small manufacturing company based in the US that needs US$20,000,000 to finance a profitable new project. The company decides to borrow this principal amount of money from a bank in the form of a five-year maturity loan. The credit grade of this company being quite poor, the bank offers a high interest rate, say 7.5 percent per annum. Metal Limited then evaluates the cost of borrowing versus the return on this new project, expected to be about 12 percent per annum. To maintain the profitability of the project, Metal Limited decides to reduce the cost of borrowing, decreasing the interest rate to be paid to the bank by providing available collateral in the form of land, machines and equipment. The bank then prices the value of this collateral, taking into account its liquidity, and decides to offer a 5 percent annual interest rate.

What is risk-free rate? This could be viewed as the interest rate that rewards Counterparty A for not using its funds in any specific project and lending them to Counterparty B, without bearing any credit risk. To make this situation possible, there should be no doubt about the trustworthiness of Counterparty B in terms of its ability and willingness to repay back its future debt obligations. Traditionally, risk-free rates were derived from Treasury rates – the rates associated with Treasury bonds issued by governments due to the "too big to fail" common belief. However, buying government bonds cannot realistically be considered free of credit risk for any given currency; history has shown that some governments have defaulted on their obligations for political and/or insolvency reasons. The Russian crisis in 1998 resulted in a default on domestic debt; and the 1999/2000 Argentine crisis hit the country's economy so hard that it caused the government to default on its foreign debt. In 2008, Greece's debt reached such a high level that the country was not able to repay its loans without external help and massive refinancing.

Interest rates depend on the type of debt issued, the covenants of the contract, its currency and the issuer's creditworthiness. Indeed, there are many debt instruments traded in the market, in the form of loans, mortgages, treasury bonds, corporate bonds, and so on. As this is the case for all kinds of financial assets, the market tends to select a specific instrument as a benchmark. For interest rates, the London Interbank Offered Rate (LIBOR) is commonly used by traders and market participants as a floating rate benchmark to assess interest rates. For example, if Australian company X issues floating rate corporate bonds denominated in US dollars to finance its future operations, the rate could be expressed as $L + 5$ percent per annum, where L refers to the three-month US Libor rate and 5 percent is the spread over Libor, giving an idea of Company X's credit grade.

LIBOR is the estimated rate at which banks borrow funds from each other. There exist many maturities for Libor rates associated with all major currencies. For instance, the Euro Libor rate associated with three-month maturity is called the Three-month EURIBOR. There is usually a spread between Libor and Treasury rates, referred to as the TED spread. Today, this spread is computed as the difference between the three-month Libor rate and the three-month treasury rate. The TED spread is expressed in basis points (bps), one basis point being equal to 0.01 percent. Its value usually fluctuates between 10 bps and 50 bps except in the case of major economic downturns. The TED spread is often used as an indicator of credit risk; as the TED spread widens, the default risk of banks increases.

Given the fact that interest rates depend on many parameters such as the type of debt, its currency and its maturity, traders and market participants need to find a solution to derive a suitable reference rate associated with their trading needs. For all major currencies, a reference graph would then be used where the associated interest rates derived from zero coupon bonds, bonds, swaps and futures are plotted against their respective maturities. These graphs are called the "yield curves." The yield curve rates are then used as a reference rate and an additional credit spread is added, its size depending on the financial transaction entered into.

Yield curves are typically upward-sloping, with shorter-term interest rates lower than longer-term interest rates. As can be seen in Figure 1.1, yield curves usually present a concave curvature; the increase in yield slows as maturities get longer. An upward-sloping curve indicates that the economy is likely to expand in the future.

Figure 1.2 shows the case where interest rates decrease as maturity increases. The yield curve is then called inverted or downward-sloping. Such yield curves reflect that the market expects lower interest rates in the future, indicating a likely slow down in the economy.

There could be cases where the shape of yield curves are humped or downward-sloping. In Figure 1.3, there is a peak at the five-year point, showing that interest rates are expected to rise during the next few years and then decrease.

There are many theories that try to explain the shape of yield curves, such as the expectations theory, the market segmentation theory and the liquidity preference theory. In practice, one should carefully examine the supply and demand relating to the different debt products traded for each currency, as interest rates are derived from these financial instruments.

Also, monetary and fiscal policies should be properly assessed, as these constitute major factors affecting the slope and curvature of the yield curve; sudden changes in

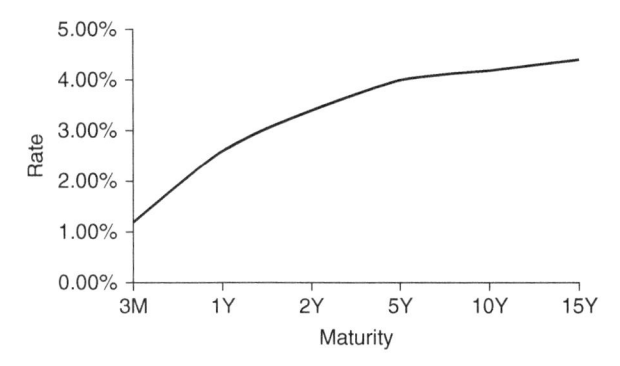

Figure 1.1 AUD denominated upward-sloping yield curve

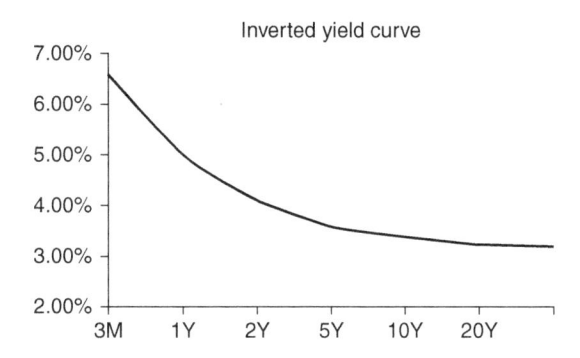

Figure 1.2 Downward-sloping curve

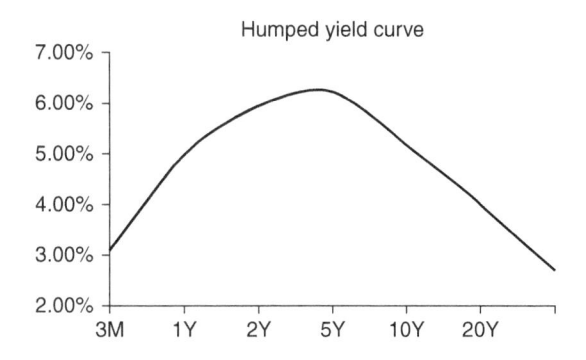

Figure 1.3 Humped yield curve

monetary and fiscal policies could have a considerable effect on the curve. Therefore, traders need to hedge their positions against these unexpected events, as they could have an adverse impact on the valuation of the portfolio depending on its sensitivity to interest rates. By using duration and convexity numbers, traders can immunize their financial positions against parallel shifts in yield curves for any given major currency.

However, they will still be exposed to non-parallel shifts in the yield curve. Depending on their own view of interest rates, traders can trade both the slope and curvature of yield curves.

In the forthcoming chapters, we will see what "primordial" interest rates do to the valuation of equity derivatives. This is due to the fact that traditional finance principles rely heavily on the concept of the time value of money, and interest rates play a key role in this theory. To explain the concept of the time value of money in simple terms, we can look at it from the following perspective. Let's assume the absence of credit risk, and that Counterparty Y would rather take possession of say GBP100,000 today than in a year's time. "Risk-free" interest could be earned on this money from today and would increase its absolute value in the future.

If Counterparty Y deposits the GBP100,000 (present value, PV) today in a safe account earning $i = 3\%$ (interest rate per annum), then the future value (FV) in one year's time would be:

$$FV = PV \times (1+i) = 100,000 \times (1+3\%) = £103,000$$

In simple terms, the time value of money can be understood as "Time increases the absolute value of money"; I insist on including the term "absolute" here, as the relative value of money, defined as its purchasing power, may decrease in the future if the inflation rate is higher than the risk-free rate.

In the formula above, we assumed interest compounded annually. Now let's assume the investor will receive a defined payoff amount, FV, at a future date T. Let i be the interest rate for this relevant period and let n denote the number of periods over which the interest is compounded. Then the present value, PV, of the future payoff can be computed as:

$$PV = \frac{FV}{(1+i)^n}$$

The formula above refers to actuarial discounting and the term $\frac{1}{(1+i)^n}$ is called the discount factor.

When pricing equity derivatives, we'll usually assume continuous compounding of interest rates, meaning that compounding occurs over an infinitesimally small period of time. We can also look at n as approaching infinity. If r is the appropriate continuously compounded interest rate and T is the maturity expressed as the number of years, then the formula above becomes:

$$PV = FV \times e^{-rT}$$

EXERCISE

An investor A holds $300,000; the USD deposit rate is flat, and equal to $r = 7\%$. If Investor A decides to deposit their $300,000, how long will it take to double this locked amount if compounding is done on a continuous basis?

Discussion

Let N denote the number of years after which Investor A's deposit becomes equal to $600,000.

Then we write the following equation:

$$FV = PV \times e^{(r \times N)}$$

Then:
$$N = \frac{\ln\left(\frac{FV}{PV}\right)}{r} = \frac{\ln\left(\frac{600{,}000}{300{,}000}\right)}{7\%} = 10 \text{ years}$$

A simple rule of thumb says that a specific amount of money doubles after circa 10 years if compounded annually at 7% interest rate.

As a general rule, the greater the risk of a debt instrument, the greater should be its expected yield. On the practical side, the higher the demand on a debt instrument, the lower its rate of return, and vice versa.

When studying equity derivatives, one should take into account the different corporate actions and events linked to the holding of the underlying stocks. Whenever these events have a strong impact on the value of the stock, they should be incorporated into the pricing formula of the associated derivative. Here, we discuss dividends which constitute an important factor in the valuation of equity derivatives.

Indeed, buying a stock entitles the holder to receive dividend payments. Under normal market conditions, the stock's price usually decreases by approximately the dividend amount on the ex-div date. And most of the time, the payoff of an equity derivative investment does not include such payments. Therefore, the pricing of an equity derivative instrument should take into account an estimation of future dividend payments that may occur during the term of the derivative.

It is very difficult, though, to estimate the value of future dividends with any degree of certainty, as this arises from corporate events decided at firm level and will depend on the firm's future strategies. Sometimes the distribution of dividends is quite stable over time, allowing some confidence in the estimated future dividends. But in the case where stocks exhibit very volatile dividend levels over time, traders tend to be very conservative when pricing associated derivatives.

Traders and market participants usually look at the stream of historical dividends to get an idea of the psychology behind their distribution. But everybody should bear in mind that market conditions may change significantly and that strategies of firms can vary accordingly. So the pricing of an equity derivative also takes into account research analysis for a specific economic sector and specialist views about a particular stock.

Dividends are usually expressed in a currency amount per stock and can also be viewed as a percentage of the stock's price. As is the case for interest rates, a continuously compounded dividend rate q can be derived. For the sake of ease of pricing, we will be mainly using this continuously compounded dividend rate as we move further into this book.

As a general rule, an equity derivative investor may not be entitled to receive any periodic interest payments, dividends or other types of cash distribution during the term of the equity derivative they invest in, and such payments may not be included in the calculation of the amount payable at maturity. Depending on the importance of their impact in the derivative's price, expected future distributions are estimated and included in the valuation formula of the stock derivative instrument.

1.3 Short Selling and Borrowing

Investors usually buy stocks because they expect the price to increase over time, so that they can make a profit from this event; they are taking a long position. But what if they believe a particular stock is overvalued? If they hold this stock, they will probably sell it and close their position to avoid expected future losses. But if they do not have this particular stock in their portfolio, how can they profit from a decline in the stock price? The answer is "short selling" – selling a stock not currently owned with the intention of buying it back later at a lower price. Speculators are not the only people motivated by going short; traders willing to hedge a long position in their portfolio may also need to short sell certain securities.

Figure 1.4 shows the different steps to be taken to achieve a short-selling strategy:
On the initial date:

- The investor borrows the shares from a broker-dealer and agrees to pay a specified borrowing fee. Collateral is also given to the lender.
- The investor immediately sells the shares on the market.

On the repurchasing date:

- The investor buys back the shares from the market.
- The investor returns back the borrowed shares to the broker.

Typically, stocks are borrowed from brokers who either hold these stocks or have them in custody on behalf of their clients. Investors can also directly borrow the stocks from large institutions such as pension funds or mutual funds, which pursue long-term strategies and are not willing to close their long positions. Lending their stocks enables those institutions to receive an additional lending fee from their current positions. Here, it is important to note that the stock borrowing process involves a title transfer of securities from the lender to the borrower, who becomes entitled to receive dividend

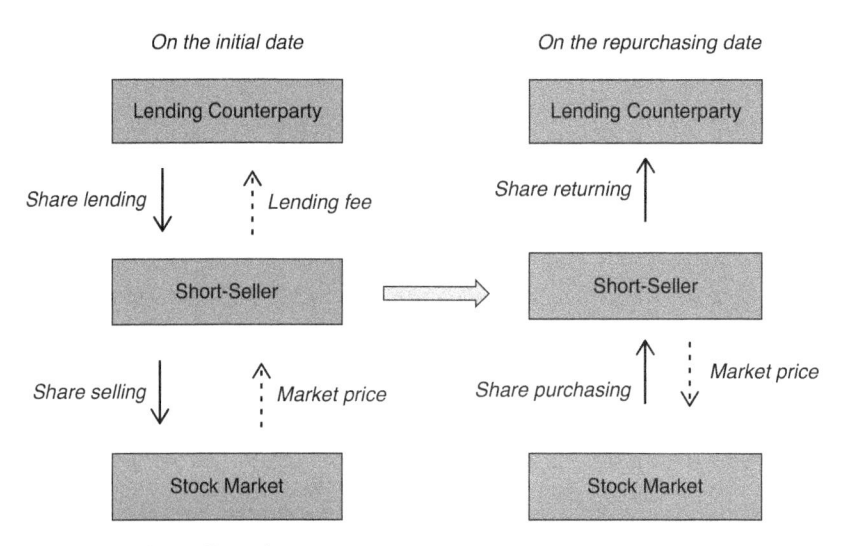

Figure 1.4 Short selling scheme

payments, for instance. Any cash payment received by the borrower during the stock loan term is usually passed back to the lender.

The most common type of stock loan is the call loan, when the lender has the option to call back their stocks and terminate the loan at any time. There are also term loans, which are less risky for the borrower, as they are set up on a specific pre-agreed period. Stock loans are governed by a Securities Lending Agreement and secured, as cash or another security is pledged as collateral. The typical borrowing rate is around 0.30 percent per annum, but this can suddenly shoot up much higher if most market participants go short on a specific stock.

EXERCISE

Amine Chkili is an equity derivatives trader working for a leading international bank. He is convinced the price of stock X is going to fall significantly in the next two months. Amine does not have this share in his portfolio and decides to short sell it. He borrows 10,000 shares through his broker and immediately sells them at $50 per share. The funds received are deposited in a safe account at 2% per annum. Compounding is assumed to be linear. Two months later, Amine's predictions have proved correct, and Stock X's price has dropped by 20%. Amine withdraws his funds to buy back the stock at the prevailing market price. Immediately afterwards, he returns the shares to the broker he initially borrowed them from. The annual lending rate is 0.30%. What was Amine's profit from this transaction?

Discussion

For a quick answer, split the calculations between the cost and revenue components for this transaction:

Costs:

- Amine buys 10,000 shares of Stock X at the market price prevailing on the repurchasing date. The stock price is equal to $50 \times (1-20\%) = \$40$.
  The repurchase cost is then equal to $10,000 \times \$40 = \$400,000$.
- Plus lending fee $= 10,000 \times \$50 \times 0.30\% \times 2/12 = \$250$.

The total cost is then equal to $400,250.

Revenues:

- Amine receives $10,000 \times \$50 = \$500,000$ from the sale of shares on the initial date.
- The interest from the deposit is circa $500,000 \times 2\% \times 2/12 = \$1667$

The total revenue is then equal to $501,667.
The resulting Profit and Loss (P&L) from this transaction is then a profit of $101,417.

Short selling involves selling a stock not currently owned. This process creates leverage and additional volatility of fluctuations in the market. Speculators may cause large downside movements in financial markets if they decide to massively short sell certain stocks. Large negative stock returns are accompanied by panic actions and could potentially lead to a market crash. Market regulators obviously work on limiting the risks of speculation and leverage on financial markets and the negative impact that this could cause to the whole economy. Therefore, many markets create restrictions on short selling. For instance, the uptick rule in the USA states that a stock is eligible to be sold short only if its last price movement was positive. In some other regulations, short selling a stock is actually banned.

1.4 Volatility Concepts

Volatility is one of the most important parameters, if not the most important, in the options valuation process. Here, we study the different types and measures of volatility when it comes to price equity options.

On looking at volatility measures using data providers such as Bloomberg or Reuters, it is important to distinguish whether it is implied or historical volatility that is displayed; either of these can be used to estimate a volatility bid or offer during a specified period of time. However, the two measures are very different in nature. Historical volatility is a statistical measure resulting in a standard deviation output, whereas implied volatility is a market parameter inferred from the prices of traded equity options.

Historical Volatility

Historical volatility uses historical prices for a particular stock to evaluate by how much the stock price returns deviate from their mean over a specified period of time.

Below is an algorithm to easily compute the standard deviation of returns σ of Stock X over a specified time period T:

1. Let $S_0, S_1, \ldots, S_n$ be the n+1 daily closing prices of Stock X during the period T.
2. For $i = 1$ to n, let R_i be the daily return defined as $R_i = \ln\left(\frac{S_i}{S_{i-1}}\right)$.
3. Compute the mean of the returns $\bar{R} = \frac{1}{n} \times \sum_{i=1}^{n} R_i$.
4. Let σ^2 be an unbiased estimate of the variance of these returns: $\sigma^2 = \frac{1}{n-1} \times \sum_{i=1}^{n} (R_i - \bar{R})^2$.
5. The standard deviation σ can then be measured as the square root of the variance.

The standard deviation computed would be a standard daily deviation, as it gives a statistical measure of how much the price returns deviate on a daily basis from its mean over the observed time period T. To compute a weekly standard deviation instead of daily, weekly price changes should be used instead of daily in point number 2 of the above algorithm. The same principle can be applied for the computation of monthly or annual standard deviation measures.

The market term, "the 90-day realized volatility for Stock A is 16%" means that the annual standard deviation computed using Stock A price data over the last 90 days is equal to 16%. Historical volatility numbers used in the market are annual standard deviations. Let σ denote the annual volatility. The volatility σ_T for a period T expressed in years is derived from the annual volatility using the following relationship:

$$\sigma_T = \sigma\sqrt{T}$$

Since historical volatility results from a statistical measure, a sufficiently large amount of data should be utilized to gain an appropriate estimate of standard deviation. It is also important to note that volatility is not constant and may vary significantly from one time period to another. Therefore, it is important to carefully select the time period over which the standard deviation measure is computed, as there may be significant regime changes.

Using ex post (past) data to make statements regarding ex ante (future) volatility may lead to potential forecasting issues. First, there are limitations to using historical estimates, when the data items are no longer relevant. Second, when forecasts fail to account for conditioning information, they may be inaccurate. "Conditioning" means that the statistical relationships were determined over a given historical time period and are naturally based on economic conditions at that time – and economic conditions can change over time; that is why historical data should not be the sole basis of forecasts.

Implied Volatility

On the other hand, implied volatility for a given stock is derived from the traded prices of options written on this particular stock. While historical volatility is inferred from past prices, implied volatility reflects the current market sentiment and expectations. Market participants mainly use implied volatility to price equity options, and can buy or sell volatility depending on whether they feel the implied volatility is under- or overvalued. The concepts behind volatility trading will be explained in more detail in the coming chapters.

Implied and historical volatility are two different types of concept; thus, it should not be surprising if these two methods lead to different volatility forecasts. However, in normal market conditions they are unlikely to differ significantly. For some illiquid stocks, however, there might not be enough written options traded frequently on the market, so it may be difficult to derive an implied volatility. In this case, traders rely on historical volatility to get an estimated number. But in any case, traders will usually consider both implied and historical volatility before giving their own quotation on volatility.

EXERCISE

Assume a historical volatility for a particular stock is equal to $\sigma = 24\%$ annually. What would be the inferred daily volatility?

Discussion

Working on the assumption that one year is equivalent to 252 business days, the daily realized volatility is computed as follows:

$$\sigma_{1d} = \frac{\sigma}{\sqrt{252}}$$

Then

$$\sigma_{1d} = \frac{24}{16} = 1.5\%$$

Skew and Term Structure of Volatility

Volatility is considered as a measure of risk, as it gives an indication of the stability level of a specific stock. When a stock is said to be very volatile, this means its prices may vary significantly over time. The higher the volatility, the greater the risk to the equity investment.

Implied volatility in the market is typically not flat, that is, volatility levels are not constant but vary depending on the maturity and strike level of the option. A "volatility surface" is a three-dimensional graph used by traders to ascertain the implied volatility of a particular stock associated with a specified strike and maturity.

For any particular stock, the skew is a graph where implied volatilities are plotted against their respective strikes for a given maturity. Figure 1.5 shows the typical shape of the skew. The strikes are expressed in percentage of the actual spot level. As strikes decrease, volatility increases. This reflects the negative correlation between stock prices and volatility. When the market moves down significantly, the additional element of fear and panic has to be costed in, as market participants start to close their long positions and drive the market even further down, causing an increase in volatility.

The volatility surface can then be viewed as a series of skews plotted against the entire range of available maturities. Let's focus now on the term structure of volatility, the graph in which volatilities are plotted against their respective maturities for a fixed strike level. This graph is usually upward-sloping, as shown in Figure 1.6, indicating higher volatility as maturity increases. In Figure 1.6, at-the-money (with strike at 100

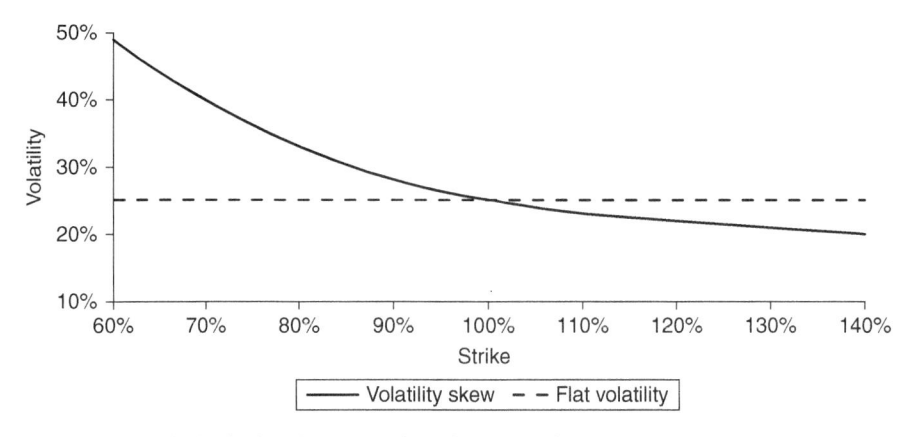

Figure 1.5 Implied volatility skew versus flat volatility graph

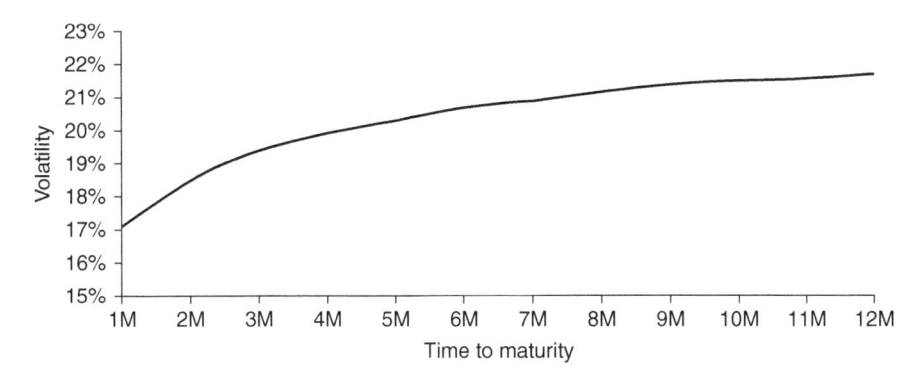

Figure 1.6 Term structure of volatility

percent) implied volatilities are plotted against time to maturity, expressed in months, for the associated traded options. But there are cases where the term structure can be downward-sloping or even exhibit a humped shape. Indeed, the market may be very nervous in the short term – due to geopolitical reasons, for instance – and could exhibit a high short-term volatility and lower volatility levels in the long run.

2 Inside the World of Equity Derivatives

2.1 The Sell Side

A Sales Story

In a bank, the sales team are the people facing the clients and discussing ideas and potential transactions with them. Sales teams represent the interface between banks or similar financial institutions and their clients. Sales teams can be segmented and organized by products and/or by geographical coverage. Meanwhile, relationship managers are, as their name implies, in charge of origination and client coverage. They are in charge of initializing and maintaining the bank's relationship with its clients. They are less specialized than salespeople, but should frequently have conversations with local and regional clients to understand their needs, and should engage the appropriate salespeople to offer the optimum solutions and continue the talks on those specific subjects.

So salespeople need to have comprehensive knowledge of the different solutions their bank can offer to its clients. They must know the products for which their bank has a competitive advantage in terms of pricing and execution, and what the bank's advantages and limitations are. Some banks may, for example, be very good at issuing and handling highly sophisticated equity derivatives, but can at the same time be much less competitive at providing a quality service and good pricing when it comes to trading vanilla (very basic and simple) products.

In contrast, equity derivatives salespeople need to be able to understand the specific needs of their clients. This is the only way they can transmit the right information to the internal technical teams in charge of providing the appropriate solution that would then be communicated to the client. It is important to note that sales teams from different financial institutions may cover the same client. The fact that a client will enter into a transaction with one financial institution instead of another depends on many factors, but one very important parameter is the quality of service received by the client.

These sales staff rely not only on information in the public domain, but also on internal research to provide their clients with new potential investment ideas. They usually take a proactive approach and engage their clients with market views and expectations. If internal research teams or the market have a directional view about a specific security or sector, then the salespeople will send research papers to their clients accompanied by derivatives products and ideas that would help the clients benefit from these potential scenarios.

There is also a marketing department to assist the salespeople. They are in charge of creating brochures about the services offered by the bank, factsheets on certain products or underlyings, and any other useful presentation for the sales teams' clients.

Salespeople usually send their clients daily factsheets and reviews about the local and global markets. This way, clients are happy to have a quick morning update on the market, but this is also an efficient sales strategy to make the clients more and more knowledgeable about their market environment. On one hand, derivatives salespeople inform their clients about the market views of some particular shares; on the other, it is even more important for them to provide their clients with education and training about the mechanics and risks of the derivatives written on these particular shares. A very important concept to understand here is that the more a client builds a personal view on a specific underlying and feels comfortable with the associated derivatives, the more they will be confident in entering into a derivatives transaction based on this underlying.

As discussed in Chapter 1, clients seeking tailored solutions trade in OTC markets and may therefore be subject to the credit risk associated with the banks they face. Clients will usually shortlist a specific number of financial companies they feel comfortable trading with from a counterparty risk perspective. Whenever clients decide to enter into an OTC transaction, they request the banks' salespeople to provide them with the costs associated with these transactions through reverse enquiries. Of the shortlisted banks, the one offering the product with the best pricing would then be chosen to trade with. If a client has an outstandingly good relationship with certain salespeople, there will be some cases where the competition is very limited or even nonexistent.

Salespeople generate commission fees for the bank whenever a financial transaction is completed. The sales fees are usually included in the pricing of the quoted financial derivative. The sales staff are usually paid a discretionary bonus at the end of the year depending on how much client income they have generated. And since the commissions are a variable rate on the notional trade value, the salespeople are often tempted to generate as many transactions as possible to increase the sales fees earned and therefore increase their end-of-year income.

However, the financial industry is regulated in such a way that all transactions must be appropriate and suitable to the client's needs. Sales staff represent the bank they work for and must at all times work in the client's best interests as long as there is no suspicion of any intent to commit financial crime. For instance, if a client asks to enter in a big notional transaction and the salesperson believes this transaction does not correspond to the client's needs, that salesperson should inform the client about the reasons why this might not be the most suitable trade even if it would have generated a large amount of commission. The most important asset in the financial world is reputation, and all market participants including salespeople must act in an ethical way, to preserve the financial industry's integrity and best practice.

Most often, an OTC transaction is accompanied by the signing of two contracts: the *termsheet* prior to the execution of the deal, and a confirmation letter once the trade has been executed. The termsheet focuses more on the terms of the transaction and skips most of formalities; the intention is to explain to the customer the technical details of the transaction they are about to enter into. The termsheet describes the transaction and explains why it constitutes a suitable and appropriate solution to the client's needs; the whole payoff formula, as well as the schedule and conditions of future cash flows, should be fully detailed so that both parties understand their obligations under the transaction.

Most investors from the buy side are by default assumed to be less financially sophisticated than sell side entities. There are many cases where customers from the buy side have refused to pay their dues and have, rightly or wrongly, accused the salespeople of having misrepresented the financial risks of a product or to have pitched a product that was not suitable for them. The main reason for such a dispute is the fact that the buy side, most often not being financial experts, have not been briefed about all the potential risks of the disputed transactions. These cases are known as "misselling."

For complex products and/or less expert investors, termsheets become more and more detailed, explaining as they do all the financial and non-financial risks arising from a transaction. They also state the governing law to be followed in case of potential disputes. Termsheets also include payout scenarios depending on the behavior of the trade underlyings – and it is recommended that they include worst case scenarios for the client, to more efficiently avoid potential misselling claims. Therefore, detailed and well designed termsheets are not only important for the client, as they will then fully understand the transaction they are entering, but termsheets also protect the banks and sellside entities from any potential misselling dispute.

From Structuring to Trading

In a bank organization, structuring teams work closely with the trading and sales teams. When the bank's clients contact the salespeople to state their hedging or yield enhancement needs, it is the structuring team that is in charge of designing the best solution and tailoring it to fit. The solution should not only meet the client's objective but must also match the client's degree of expertise. The range of complexity for equity derivatives varies from vanilla to exotic products; vanilla products are the easiest to understand, whereas exotic derivatives have the most complex payout mechanisms. Therefore, structuring teams in partnership with salespeople must assess the degree of client's sophistication before deciding on the most suitable solution. Indeed, one of the most important rules in the OTC derivatives world is to make the proposed transaction understandable to the client. Even if an exotic financial product is the best answer to the client's request, if the client does not have enough expertise in the derivatives field to understand it such a product should not be offered.

Structuring teams can be linked with product innovation. Structurers not only work on reverse enquiries from the clients, but also are in charge of continuously giving birth to new financial products in the market. They usually work closely with traders and the bank's risk functions, to assess whether their newfound idea is consistent with the bank's strategy and to ascertain whether the trading teams can book this financial product. This will mostly depend on the trading team's capability in terms of hedging and controlling the risks inherent in the newly proposed solution. When creating a new product for the bank, structuring teams will engage the front-to-back chain within the bank; this includes legal, compliance, tax, middle office, back office and accounting departments. When all these teams are comfortable with the new product and all its financial and non-financial risks are understood and manageable, then the structurers will issue a new presentation for the salespeople; they brief them on the benefits and risks of this new solution, who the target clients are, etc.

Structuring teams are usually engaged at the inception of a potential transaction. As discussed, they come up with different solutions and adjust them as conversations with the client evolve and as all the client's objectives and constraints become fully understood. A big transaction may take months to close, and salespeople do not hesitate to put structurers up in front of the client during their meetings; the idea is to come up with the most suitable product, and also to be able to more easily set up the background of a new idea, which is better understood by the structurer. A good structuring team is one of the key selling points for salespeople, presenting a great image of the bank in terms of sophistication and innovation; it shows how the bank is capable of offering its clients the best tailored solutions in the market.

Structuring teams must have sales skills in that they should be able to perfectly understand the clients' objectives and constraints but should also be able to explain technical solutions in a language understandable by the clients. They can partner with salespeople to prepare termsheets or presentations for customers. They can also work with marketers to produce new brochures. Clients can engage structurers directly to understand a financial transaction or discuss a specific market situation and potential opportunities. Apart from the level of sales commissions, every financial product has a price linked to its hedging costs. Indeed, when a product is offered, it goes onto the book of traders who are in charge of hedging its risks on a day-to-day basis until the transaction reaches maturity. Structuring and trading teams together price the financial solution before the trade is closed. During the life of a transaction, clients usually ask for indicative prices for their OTC derivatives, and structurers will most often give this pricing. Traders then give the final price when a client is ready to trade. This price corresponds to the cost of hedge. This is a very important concept to understand, and it will be explored in greater depth later in this book.

So structurers can be seen as assessing all the risks inherent to a transaction prior to its inception, and traders will manage these risks during the life of the trade. A good structuring team cannot shine without a good trading team. Indeed, price is a key factor when trading equity derivatives. Even if an idea offered to the client is perfect for them, its cost or price must be competitive, or the client may well ask another bank for the same idea if they feel they can get a better price for it. Also, original and sophisticated new products are usually derivatives that are difficult to hedge, so a smarter trader will be needed in order to successfully handle these risks. We are not talking about proprietary traders here, that is traders that have a budget to grow the bank's portfolio depending on their own speculative market views. When we discuss trading teams from the sell side, this mostly consists of the exotic and vanilla trading desks in charge of hedging the associated books and therefore supporting the bank's derivatives business.

Structuring teams can also be seen as the link between sales and trading; they create a link between the marketing side and the risk/hedging side. If a salesperson receives a reverse enquiry, where many banks are competing to price an investment product for instance, he or she sends the request to structurers and traders and expects the trading teams to come up with the best pricing to win the auction and increase sales. Traders will try to give the best possible price depending on their ability to perform the hedge for the quoted product as well as the estimated cost of hedge. Sales usually win or lose

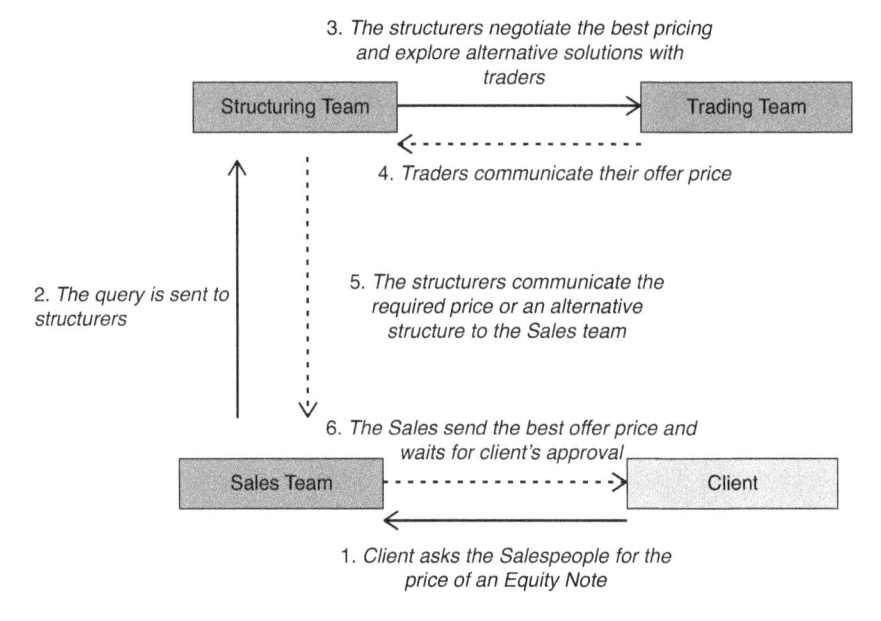

Figure 2.1 Communication scheme between the sell side front office and the buy side when a reverse enquiry takes place

Diagram flow:
- 1. Client asks the Salespeople for the price of an Equity Note
- 2. The query is sent to structurers
- 3. The structurers negotiate the best pricing and explore alternative solutions with traders
- 4. Traders communicate their offer price
- 5. The structurers communicate the required price or an alternative structure to the Sales team
- 6. The Sales send the best offer price and waits for client's approval

some trades and may express their frustration towards trading desks when they bring the client to the auction table and never win it. Structurers will then facilitate the communication between the two desks, explaining why the trading desk cannot be competitive for a certain product. They could also give guidance on alternative products where the bank is competitive and which have the potential to generate better revenues.

There is always a general potential for disagreements between the sales and trading teams, given that the sales team is focused on increasing revenues and the trading team has additional concerns, namely to assess and perform its risk management functions. On the other hand, traders benefit from the existence of flow trades, which consists of the standard transactions brought in by sales team that are characterized by a high trading frequency and consistency. Indeed, having a flow business enables the traders to put less effort into hedging their books as the hedge process and booking models become standardized. Also, matching bids and asks is very beneficial to the business, as hedging costs may decrease significantly. And since the fair price of a derivative is equal to its cost of hedge, then traders can be more aggressive in the way their quoted prices are more competitive. Here, we understand how all front office functions are linked, as all functions are dependent on each other to perform well. No matter what may be said in the market, teamwork will always do the job better.

Risk Control Mechanisms

So far, we have extensively discussed the roles and the importance of the various front office functions. But one of the most essential departments within a bank is the risk management office; it is responsible for ensuring that the risk policies that have been decided at senior management level are being appropriately implemented by the individual operational units. When any portfolio or trading book is created, its risk and return objectives are clearly defined. In addition, the portfolio time to maturity, liquidity constraints, tax environment, regulations and unique circumstances must be specified.

Banks, insurance companies, hedge funds, pension funds and other important financial institutions must comply with the rules of the regulators. The idea is to protect the integrity of the financial system by preventing any breach of compliance laws and regulations. It is very important to understand the great importance of an ethical financial system. Indeed, if the people lose faith in the financial system, there will be no more investments, and the whole sector will collapse catastrophically. We all know the disastrous consequences this will have on the whole economy and society. That's why all financial institutions must put in place strict control mechanisms to protect the clients and foster their confidence in the financial sector. The solution comes through acting in good faith and complying with the rules set out by the board of directors and senior management.

In a bank for example, every part of the risk management department is in charge of a particular aspect of risk. It is the duty of the personnel concerned to put risk control mechanisms and processes in place, in order to identify any breach of risk limits and find an appropriate solution in a timely fashion. Each equity derivatives trader has their own limits, depending on their experience and the objectives and constraints of the book they are managing. As diversification reduces risk, there are usually limits in terms of exposure to a single stock or to a specific sector. This enables the financial institution not to put all its eggs in the same basket; the bank must survive even if one company goes bankrupt or one sector collapses. More generally, the portfolio sensitivities to the different market parameters such as stock prices, interest rates, dividends, and volatility must be controlled and should lie within predefined ranges, again according to how the book's risk and return features have been designed.

The idea here is to put a number to the risk of a trading book, as this is an efficient way to specify targets and limits. Among the most popular measures designed to quantify portfolio risk, we find volatility and Value at Risk (VaR). In order to quantify and control market and price risk exposure within major financial organizations, the VaR is often used as the primary measure, as it is the basis for most market risk capital calculations. The VaR identifies the mark-to-market loss that a portfolio or set of portfolios can suffer during a specified period (daily, weekly, monthly . . .) at a predetermined confidence level. Limits are usually defined, such as the VaR will not reach a threshold level above which senior management is not comfortable with the risk of the trading book. VaR is usually complemented by a supplementary set of non-VaR limits. These limits are tailored to meet the unique needs of each business, and may include Greek measures, net open positions, tenor or gross trading limits.

2.2 The Buy Side

Corporate Clients

Traditionally, corporate needs for derivatives are most often linked to hedging. Companies will usually enter into derivatives contracts to gain protection against fluctuations of interest rates, currencies or commodities. Indeed, the use of debt in the form of corporate bonds for instance, to finance new projects, investments or operating expenses, creates an exposure to interest rates. Companies will therefore use interest rate swaps or other types of derivative to modify this exposure according to their view and needs. Foreign exchange derivatives are often linked to import and export operations; airlines will enter into commodities derivatives to hedge their fuel oil purchases, and mining companies may feel the need to protect themselves against decreasing prices in the metal asset they are producing.

Corporates are considered the most important clients for the banks' commodity, interest rates and FX derivatives desks, as their hedging needs involve large notional transactions. This is not always the case in the equity derivatives world, as this need for hedging is much more difficult to identify. However, equity derivatives salespeople will still target the treasury departments of big corporate clients to enhance the potential yield from their excess cash. Most of the time, companies put their excess cash to work through Repurchase Agreements, also known as Overnight Investments. This way, the company's available funds are lent to produce extra income. Overnight investments are very secure and highly liquid, and have a fully automated process that is not time-consuming for the treasury department.

Corporates are not risk takers. Their function is not to create wealth by speculating in financial markets; their main objective is to be able to do the business they were originally intended to do. Cash management is only a way to generate a slightly higher return, by putting every available dollar to work. Equity derivatives salespeople will therefore try to optimize this treasury management process by offering principal protected solutions that comply with the high liquidity and credit constraints and at the same time offer a potentially higher variable return linked to a specified equity underlying. It is important to note that corporates should not be treated as financial experts, so they are interested in vanilla products whose payoff mechanism is clear, and easily understood.

In Chapter 7, we discuss yield enhancement solutions in more detail. We will explore why clients are in need of principal protected notes, and how equity structured notes are built and priced. We will also study other products offered essentially for speculation purposes, and how these solutions offer not only risk control mechanisms but also an expected yield greater than the risk-free rate.

Retail and Institutional Investors

Retail Investors

Retail investors could be asset management companies or even banks that buy structured financial products issued by other banks and redistribute them to private investors or their individual clients. In short, retail investors do not have the technology to build and hedge products, but they do have enough marketing tools. Retail investors are the high street banks; they are well represented and can reach a large population. The nominal amounts are much lower than the notionals found in the financial markets, but the number of individual investors is potentially much higher.

The structured products offered to the public are usually capital guaranteed with a variable payoff linked to equity underlyings. So the invested capital is usually safe and there could be a potentially large equity-linked payoff. The clients of retail banks are assumed to have the lowest degree of sophistication. This means the risks of the offered structured investments should be properly defined and carefully explained.

Retail investors are not willing to take on the market risk of the built structured products. Either they do not have enough technology to hedge these products or they adopt a strategy in which they do not want to manage these risks. Instead of offering and hedging these products themselves, they prefer to buy them from other banks and re-offer them to individual investors with a higher price including their sales fees.

Institutional Investors

Institutional investors can be hedge funds, pension funds, insurance companies, asset management companies, family offices, private investors and even proprietary trading desks within banks. Institutional investors can be classified as speculators; their main objective is to read the market accurately and get new information that enables them to create wealth. Hedging companies, in contrast, need to protect their wealth.

Institutional investors are usually considered sophisticated investors. They have more expertise in financial markets, and they trade according to specific strategies. They are knowledgeable about the latest market news and updates, and are in continuous search for new information to try and outperform the market. Most often, institutional investors do their own research based on the existing papers and updates available on the market.

They infer market scenarios during specific future periods and intend to maximize their gain should these scenarios prove to be true. Most of the time, these scenarios have accurate parameters. For instance, they might be willing to invest in a product that would enable them to take profit from a scenario where the performance of the CAC 40 index would vary in the range (-7%; 6.5%) over the upcoming two months. Therefore, structurers in banks work on offering them the product most likely to maximize their gain if this scenario proves to be true, and which would be in line with their specific expressed constraints. Institutional investors are the clients that invest in exotic products; for most of them, vanilla products would be less suitable.

3 Forwards, Futures and Swaps

3.1 Futures Markets

Stock futures are standardized contracts where two counterparties agree to exchange a specified number of underlying stocks for a pre-agreed price (the futures price) with delivery and payment on a specified future date, the delivery date. In a futures contract, the party buying the underlying stock in the future is said to be long, while the seller is referred to as being short. These financial contracts are negotiated and traded in futures exchanges, which play an intermediary role between the long and short counterparties.

Single stock futures are often marketed in batches of 100 and are commonly traded in various financial markets. Equity futures contracts can also be based on the performance of stock indices. For example, portfolio managers trade large notionals of futures contracts based on the S&P 500 index on a daily basis in the US futures markets. Index futures contracts represent the right and obligation to buy or sell a portfolio of stocks characterized by their index. For each index, there is an associated multiplier number in the futures contract that is associated with that particular index. The value of the index futures contract is then defined as the multiplier times the price of the index underlying.

In a futures contract, the buyer and the seller are both committed to fulfill their payments obligations. As it is often the case for delta-one products, equity futures are said to be zero-sum game financial instruments, as they specify the characteristics of a future trade where the profit of one party is equal to the loss of the other party. To close out a futures position prior to the settlement date, one must take the opposite position in another exchange-traded futures contract with the same underlying asset, specified quantity and settlement date. The profit and loss is then computed using the difference in futures prices.

Let's take the example of an investor who takes a long position in 700 futures contracts based on the Euro Stoxx 50 with a delivery date of six months ahead. At the trade inception, the value of the underlying index is equal to €2300. The associated multiplier from the contract specifications is 10. Then the value of one contract at the initial date is equal to 10 × €2300 euros: €23,000. Two weeks later, the index has moved in favor of the investor, increasing in value to €2520. The investor then decides to close his position and lock his gains. He does this by taking the opposite position in the same futures. In our example, the investor goes short the futures on the same underlying with the same maturity date. The value of one contract rose to 10 × €2520 = €25,200. Therefore the total profit can be computed as 700 × (€25,200 − €23,000) = €1,540,000.

The two methods of delivery covered by single stocks futures trading are physical delivery and cash settlement. In physically delivered futures contracts, the long counterparty must buy the underlying stock from the short upon maturity of the contract; also, physical delivery requires additional work to be done to guarantee the actual delivery of the underlying stock. It is a popular settlement method in the world of bonds and commodities, but is much less frequent in the equity business. The cash delivery alternative requires the long and short parties to settle by making a cash payment based on the calculated profit and loss when the futures contract expires. It is important to note that futures written on stock market indexes are all cash-settled contracts; there is no such thing as physical delivery for a stock index.

Once a trade has been executed on a liquid futures exchange, it is almost immediately handed over to a clearing house that stands between the long and short counterparties and becomes responsible to all members for the fulfillment of the contracts. Entering into a futures contract does not require a cash investment *per se*. However, the exchange allocates margin accounts to both parties and requires them to deposit an initial cash amount, referred to as "initial margin." This amount is set by the exchange, and computed based on the maximum estimated daily movement in the futures contract value. The initial margin will typically vary between 5 percent and 15 percent of the total exposure. This allows investors to create leverage using futures contracts.

In order to emphasize the leverage effect when dealing on derivatives, let's take the example of an investor who has a bullish view on Stock X for the next two months. Let's also assume that the market price of Stock X at $t = 0$ is equal to \$100 per share, and the two-month futures price is equal to \$101.5 per share. Now, let's consider two scenarios. In the first, the investor buys 1000 shares of Stock X at $t = 0$ and two months later sells back 1000 shares at \$1200 per share. The return for this transaction is as follows:

$$return = \frac{1,000 \times 120}{1,000 \times 100} - 1 = 20\%$$

In the second scenario, the investor chooses to enter at $t = 0$ into a long position in 1000 futures written on Stock X with a two-month maturity. We assume the initial margin (initial investment) is equal to \$5100. Two months later, the futures price is equal to the market price of \$120 per share. The bullish view of the investor proved to be correct and they receives their initial margin plus the profit from the long futures position, that is $5100 + 1000 \times (120 - 101.5) = \$23,600$. If we compute the return on this investment, we get the following:

$$return = \frac{23,600}{5,100} - 1 = 363\%$$

Here we see the effect of leverage. Using a much lower investment, an investor can make a similar dollar profit using derivatives. It is important to note, however, that leverage not only magnifies the return but also magnifies the risk.

On a daily basis, the change in the future's price from one day to another is used to compute the profit and loss to be withdrawn from the margin account of one counterparty and credited to the margin account of the other counterparty. This same mechanism is repeated daily until the expiry date of the futures contract. For example, if the price of a single stock future contract appreciates from one day to another, the

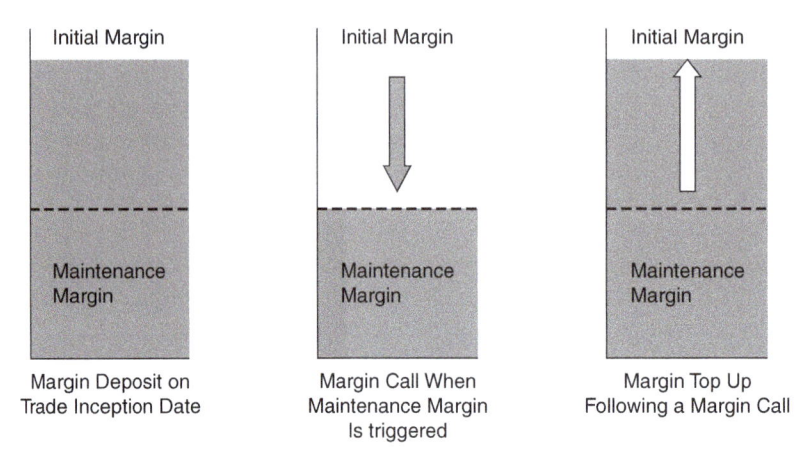

Figure 3.1 Margin call mechanism

exchange or clearing house will put the corresponding amount of money into the margin account of the long counterparty. The same amount will be debited from the margin account of the short counterparty, and vice versa.

Figure 3.1 illustrates the case where the margin account of one of the parties depreciates in value until it reaches a preset maintenance margin. Once this minimum level is triggered, a margin call is issued and the counterparty has to inject enough money to bring the account back up to the initial margin. Often referred to as a variation margin, the margin called is expected to be paid and received on a daily basis. Otherwise, the counterparty's broker can at their discretion close sufficient positions at the market price so that the required funds are available in the margin account. This entire process is referred to as marking-to-market.

Two types of market actors are mainly involved in the equity futures business: hedgers and speculators. Hedgers seek to decrease their portfolio risk by decreasing their price exposure to a particular equity underlying. Pension funds, insurance companies or other hedge funds which are willing to decrease an existing exposure to a single stock, a basket of stocks or a particular stock index, can use equity futures to do so. They would partially or totally offset their actual exposure to a specific underlying over a certain period of time by taking an opposite position in a corresponding notional of futures contracts. In the very rare cases where the manager's portfolio exactly reflects a specific index, it could then be perfectly hedged during a particular period by shorting the index future contract. As long as the futures contract's position is still open, the exposure to the underlying index is neutralized, that is, the movements in the price of the index do not have any impact on the portfolio's performance. Instead, the portfolio manager earns the risk-free rate during the hedging period. It is important to note that portfolios are most often partially hedged using a proxy index future that has a high degree of correlation with the target portfolio.

Alternatively, portfolio managers or proprietary traders can enter into futures contracts to increase their exposure to a particular stock or index. In the case of speculators, the long counterparty in a futures contract expects to make a profit from their position in the scenario of an increase in the underlying's price, but would otherwise suffer a loss. The opposite applies for the short counterparty. Speculators can create leverage using a futures contract. Also they can easily decide to make profit out of a bearish market by shorting futures, since futures are not subject to the sort of selling limitations that stocks have to abide by. An index futures is a very common and popular financial instrument that enables speculators to gain exposure to a broad market index – an index, which is a formula and not an investment vehicle, cannot be bought or sold directly.

More generally, equity futures contracts are very useful when it comes to transferring the risk of an equity underlying from counterparty to another. They are easy to use and provide the equity markets with increased liquidity between market participants that have their own constraints and different risk and return objectives. It is also important to note that entering into an equity future only provides the investor with the price exposure of the stock underlying, that is, there are no additional benefits, such as dividends or voting rights, associated with holding the stock.

Now that we have discussed the mechanism and advantages of using futures contracts, let's look at how we can evaluate the theoretical futures price specified in a single stock futures contract. Let F be the theoretical futures price of stock X at time T, and S the current spot price. For pricing purposes, we assume a continuous dividend yield q, a continuous risk-free interest rate r, no transaction costs, identical borrowing and lending costs, and no restrictions on short selling. The theoretical forward price specified in equity futures contracts is equal to:

$$F = S \times e^{(r-q)T}$$

Let's keep in mind that the fair price is the theoretical price such that there can be no arbitrage opportunity. Let's assume that an investor is bullish on a specific stock X paying a dividend yield equal to q. Also, let's assume the interest rates are equal to r. From a profit standpoint based on a period T (expressed in number of years), there should be no difference between buying the stock or entering into a long position written on this stock with a maturity T. To replicate/hedge the long forward position, a trader can borrow an amount equal to the initial stock price S at rate r during period T. They then buy Stock X with the borrowed cash and hold it. During that period, they receive a dividend yield equal to q for being the stock holder. The total equivalent cost for this operation (in percentage terms) is equal to $(r-q)$. At the maturity date, the trader sells the stock to the long counterparty at the pre-agreed forward price, and repays their loan. In order not to create any arbitrage opportunity, the pre-agreed forward price at initial date must be equal to the cost of hedging or replicating the forward, that is, $F = S \times e^{(r-q)T}$.

In a perfect market, the relationship between futures and spot prices depends only on the above variables; but in practice there are various market imperfections (transaction costs, differential borrowing and lending rates, restrictions on short selling) that prevent complete arbitrage. Thus, the futures price in fact varies, within arbitrage boundaries, around the theoretical price. A smart way to remember whether there should be a positive or negative sign before any of the formula parameters is to ask whether this parameter is a cost (the borrowing interest rate) or a benefit (the dividends received); there is a positive sign when it is a cost, and a negative sign when there is a benefit.

3.2 Forward Contracts

Equity forwards are agreements between two counterparties to buy/sell a specific quantity of an agreed equity underlying at a given future date at a guaranteed price K (also called the "strike price"). The underlying could be a stock, a basket of stocks or a given stock index. Equity forwards are typically OTC products and are not traded on exchanges. These contracts are not standardized and are designed to fit the needs of clients exactly. Moreover, there are no cash exchanges due to marking-to-market until the contract's maturity date.

Figure 3.2 shows the main product technical terms specified in a forward termsheet: the underlying security, the strike price and the maturity date. At that date, the spot of the underlying equity is observed, to determine the contract's payoff. The settlement date is the payment day when the cash is transferred between the two counterparties, and is usually two business days after the maturity date.

Most often, equity forwards are cash-settled instruments. At expiry date, the payoff is equal to the difference between the underlying's spot price and the pre-agreed strike price. If the equity underlying's market price observed at maturity is above the strike price, then the buyer (the long counterparty) receives from the seller (the short counterparty) the price difference times the specified quantity.

Let S_T be the spot price of the underlying security at maturity date T and let N be the specified quantity in the termsheet. The payoff from the forward contract is as follows:

- $\text{Payoff}_{\text{long forward}} = N \times \{S_T - K\}$ for the long position
- $\text{Payoff}_{\text{short forward}} = N \times \{K - S_T\}$ for the short position

Figure 3.3 shows the payoff patterns of long and short positions in forward contracts. The graphs emphasize the delta-one features of forwards, as the profit of the long counterparty is equal to the loss of the short counterparty. At any given point in time, the difference between the spot price and the strike price is called the "forward premium" or "forward discount," depending on whether this difference is positive or negative.

Buyer	Counterparty L
Seller	Counterparty S
Underlying Asset	Bouygues
Number of Shares	100,000
Currency	EUR
Initial Spot Price	20, 40
Strike Price	21, 30
Initial Date	May 15, 2013
Maturity Date	May 14, 2014
Settlement Date	May 16, 2014
Delivery Method	Cash

Figure 3.2 Terms of a one-year forward contract

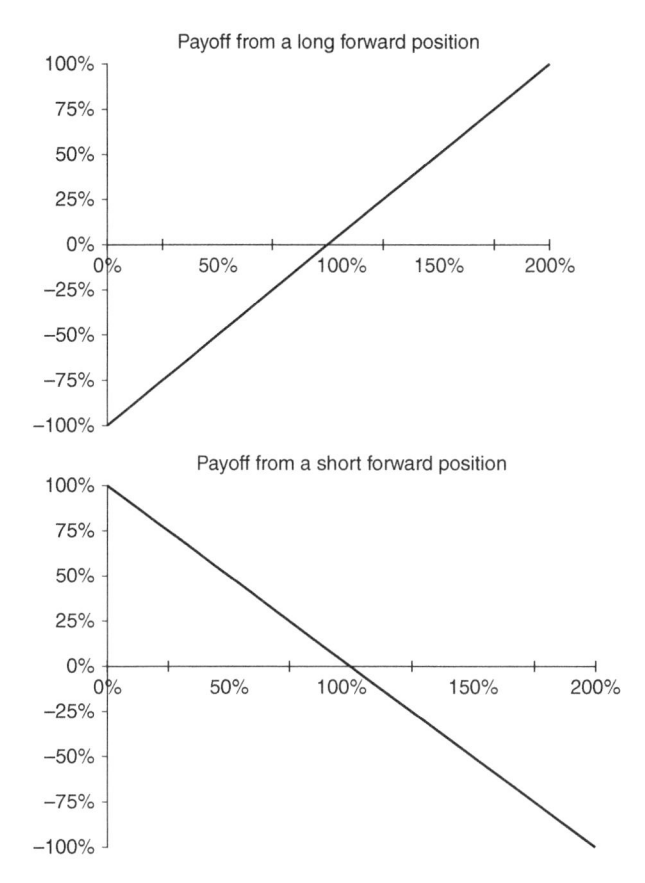

Figure 3.3 Payoff patterns from long and short forward positions

Let's take the trade example set out in Figure 3.2. At the trade inception, Counterparty S was the short counterparty and wanted to lock the offer price of Bouygues 100,000 shares at €2,130,000 in one year's time, to raise some cash. At the maturity date, if the observed market price of Bouygues is equal to €25.10, then Counterparty S owes counterparty L a cash amount equal to 100,000 × (€25.10 − €21.30) = €380,000, to be paid on the settlement date. Now if the observed price at maturity is equal to €18.30, then Counterparty S would receive from Counterparty L a payoff equal to 100,000 × (€21.30 − €18.30) = €300,000. Very importantly, the payoff is equal to the total profit in the case of forwards, since the only cash exchange during the life of the contract is made at the settlement date.

Like futures trading, forward contracts can be used for hedging or speculation purposes. As previously mentioned, the equity underlying could be a stock, an index or a basket of stocks. Let's consider the case of a portfolio manager willing to buy a list of securities at a given date in the future. If the investor wants to hedge against a market price increase, they could enter into a long position in forward contracts written on each of these stocks. But this solution is very costly in terms of fees. Instead, the portfolio manager could enter into one forward contract on a basket of stocks which gives the same payoff but is much cheaper from a fees standpoint.

Now let's talk about a fund that exactly mimics the performance of the S&P 500 index. If the fund manager wants to protect the $7,000,000 value of their portfolio for the next three months, they can contact their broker to get a quote on a forward contract for $7,000,000, to sell the index. At the expiry date, if the portfolio has dropped by 2.5%, the fund loses $2.5\% \times \$7,000,000 = \$175,000$. In theory, the index would have decreased by 2.5% if we assume the portfolio has followed the index perfectly. Then the fund manager gains $2.5\% \times \$7,000,000 = \$175,000$ from the short position in the index forward contract. The hedge is efficient, as the loss from the portfolio is offset by the gain from the position in the forward contract.

The strike price is quoted at the trade date and is theoretically equal to the forward price so that the contract's value is equal to zero. This way, there is no cash exchange at inception date. As we explained in Chapter 1, the theoretical forward price is equal to:

$$F = S \times e^{(r-q)T}$$

The price or value of a forward contract is equal to the present value of the expected payoff at maturity. From the long counterparty standpoint, the payoff is as follows:

$$\text{Payoff}_{\text{longforward}} = N \times \{S_T - K\}$$

Then at any point of time t, the expected payoff is equal to:

$$\text{Expected Payoff}_{\text{longforward}}(t) = N \times \left\{ S_t \times e^{(r-q)\times(T-t)} - K \right\}$$

This expected payoff is discounted at the risk-free rate to get the value of the forward contract from the long counterparty perspective:

$$\text{Forward}_{\text{long}}(t) = N \times \left\{ S_t \times e^{(r-q)\times(T-t)} - K \right\} \times e^{-r\times(T-t)}$$

By simplifying, we get:

$$\text{Forward}_{\text{long}}(t) = N \times \left\{ S_t \times e^{-q\times(T-t)} - K \times e^{-r\times(T-t)} \right\}$$

Forward contracts are delta-one products. This implies that the value of a forward contract from the short counterparty standpoint is equal to the opposite:

$$\text{Forward}_{\text{short}}(t) = N \times \left\{ K \times e^{-r\times(T-t)} - S_t \times e^{-q\times(T-t)} \right\}$$

Note that at inception date the value of a forward contract is equal to zero for $K = S_0 \times e^{(r-q)T}$, which is the futures price:

$$\text{Forward}_{\text{long}}(0) = N \times \left\{ S_0 \times e^{(-q\times T)} - K \times e^{(-r\times T)} \right\}$$
$$= N \times \left\{ S_0 \times e^{(-q\times T)} - S_0 \times e^{(r-q)\times T} \times e^{(-r\times T)} \right\} = 0$$

Equity futures and forwards may seem to be very similar instruments, in that they are both used to buy or sell an equity underlying asset on a future date at a pre-agreed price. However, they differ in many aspects. First, futures are standardized contracts while forwards are traded over the counter and can be tailored to fit clients' needs. But more importantly, forwards have no margining process and there is only a single payment, made at the very end of the life of the contract. The absence of clearing house and thus margin requirements means that both counterparties in a forward contract face each other directly. Therefore, the credit risk is much higher in the case of forwards whereas it is almost null for futures trading. Here we clearly understand the role of the clearing house, which consists of minimizing the counterparty risk, and this enables traders to exchange futures without having to perform extensive due diligence on their counterparty. Also, the clearing house could reduce settlement risks by netting offsetting transactions, by monitoring collateral and by providing a guaranteed fund to meet the losses in case of default events.

Let's take the example of a six-month contract on Bouygues with a price of €22. Let's say that on Day 16 another futures contract written on the same underlying with the same expiry date costs €22.40. On Day 17, let's say the futures contract costs €22.70. Then the mark-to-market process requires the short counterparty to post €0.30 of margin that is wired via margin accounts to the long counterparty. Then in the case of futures profit and loss is realized on a daily basis, whereas for forward contracts it is not realized until the expiry date. Note that this mark-to-market process creates a difference in practice between forward and futures prices when interest rates are stochastic; but this difference does not exist in the case of deterministic interest rates.

3.3 Equity Swaps

An equity swap is a pure OTC derivative contract where two counterparties agree to exchange future cash flows according to a preset schedule. In an equity swap, at least one of the cash flows is linked to an equity performance. The underlying here could be a stock, a basket of stocks or an equity index. This is commonly referred as the "equity leg." The other swap leg most often involves a fixed- income cash flow pegged to a market interest rate such as LIBOR. But this is not always the case, as there are many variations as to what constitutes the other leg; some equity swaps exist with an equity leg versus a fixed rate leg, and others even exist with two equity legs. As in plain vanilla swaps, there is a single notional principal and a specified tenor for equity swaps.

Let's take the example of Charaf Echatbi, who is part of an equity swaps Delta-One trading desk and has been approached by one of his clients to exchange the capital gains from the S&P500 index against a floating-rate calculated based on a $10 million notional. Charaf quotes the following, assuming a swap tenor of 180 days:

The Bank swaps $10 million at 6m LIBOR + 20bps against the return of the S&P equity index based on the agreed notional. Let's assume the S&P500 index had appreciated by 8% since trade inception after six months and the LIBOR rate is equal to 5% per annum, then after 180 days the swap cash flows are as follows:

The bank pays to the client an interest payment of (5% + 0.20%) × $10,000,000 × 180/360 = $260,000.

On the same date, the client pays to the bank an equity-linked payoff of 8% × $10,000,000 = $800,000.

Let's remember that swaps are purely OTC products and can be customized to fit each client's needs in a very specific fashion. In our examples, we consider the cases where there are no dividend payments. Total return equity swaps are swaps that pay the equity leg receiver an additional cash amount equivalent to the underlying's dividend payments.

$1 million based on S&P

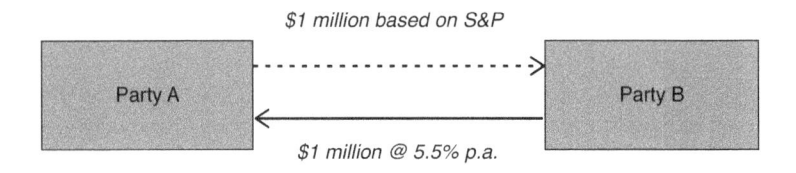

Party A → Party B

$1 million @ 5.5% p.a.

Party A ← Party B

At maturity date:

$1,000,000*3% = $30,000
Equity based payoff

Party A ← Party B

Interest Payment
$1,000,000*5.5%*90/360 = $13,750

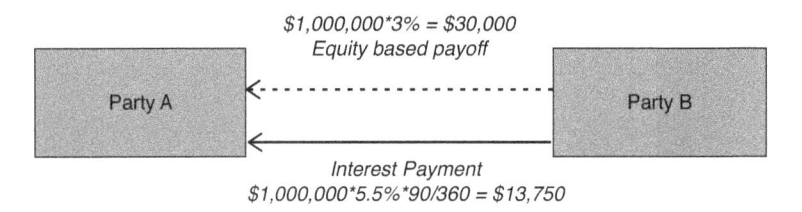

Party A ← Party B

Figure 3.4 Cash flows exchanged in a three-month bullet equity swap

The payment is usually netted where the bank receives $800,000 − $260,000 = $540,000. In this particular example, there is only a single payment, made on the maturity of the swap. When this is the case, the equity swap is referred to as a "bullet equity swap."

Also it is very important to note that the equity leg receiver gets the positive or negative return of the equity benchmark. This means that if the performance is positive they receive money, but if the equity return is negative they owe an equity payoff in addition to the interest payment. Figure 3.4 shows cash flows exchanged in a three-month bullet equity swap where Party A is an equity index payer and fixed rate receiver. In this example, we assume a fixed annual interest rate of 5.5%, and notional is $1,000,000.

At the maturity of the swap (after 90 days), if the S&P500 index had depreciated by 3%, then Party A would actually receive $30,000 for the negative equity return on top of the fixed interest payment.

EXERCISE

An investor A holds £20,000,000 of Stock X. They believe Stock X will underperform in the next six months and want to hedge their current exposure for that period of time. At the same time, Investor A wants to obtain equity return exposure to another Stock, Y, for the next six months. Investor A decides to enter into an equity swap with Bank C. James Cook is an equity swap trader working for Bank C; he finds an Investor, B, willing to enter into the opposite transaction. James Cook quotes two equity swaps with £20,000,000 notional and six months' tenor, as shown below.

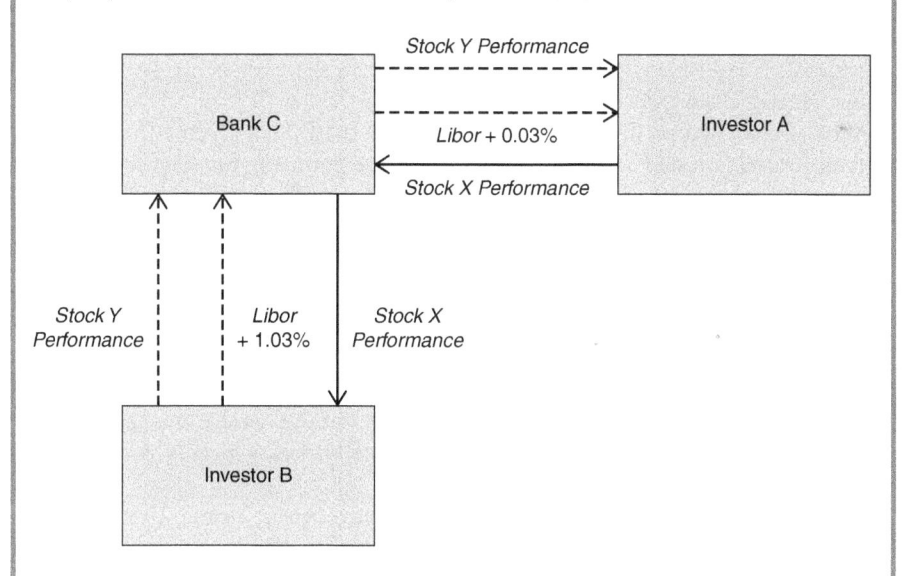

```
                    Stock Y Performance
         ┌─────────────────────────────────→
         │
    ┌─────────┐    Libor + 0.03%         ┌──────────┐
    │         │─────────────────────────→│          │
    │ Bank C  │                          │Investor A│
    │         │←─────────────────────────│          │
    └─────────┘    Stock X Performance   └──────────┘
       ↑  ↑    │
       │  │    │
   Stock Y │  Libor    Stock X
 Performance │ +1.03%  Performance
       │  │    │
       │  │    ↓
    ┌─────────┐
    │Investor B│
    └─────────┘
```

After 180 days (swap tenor), Stock X has performed by 7% whereas Stock Y has performed by 2.5%. We assume a LIBOR rate of 1.07% per annum. What would be the P&L (Profit and Loss) of each of the three counterparties?

Discussion

Investor A:
Investor A owes £20,000,000 × 7% = £1,400,000 to Bank C
  Bank C owes £20,000,000 × {2.5% + (1.07% + 0.03%) × 180/360} = £610,000 to Investor A.
  P&L for Investor A is then equal to £610,000 − £1,400,000 = £790,000

Investor B:
Bank C owes £20,000,000 × 7% = £1,400,000 to Investor B
  Investor B owes £20,000,000 × {2.5% + (1.07% + 1.03%) × 180/360} = £710,000 to Bank C
  P&L for Investor B is then equal to £1,400,000 − £710,000 = £690,000

Bank C:
Here we note that Bank C has hedged its price exposure through these two swap transactions. All the floating payments offset each other and the P&L for Bank C is independent of market movements. It is always equal to 1.03% − 0.03% = 1% p.a., i.e. £20,000,000 × 1% × 180/360 = £100,000.
  It is important to note that although the price is hedged here, Bank C is still exposed to credit risk with respect to both Investor A and B. Swaps are zero-sum game financial instruments, so an easy calculation check is to compute the sum of P&Ls and verify that it is equal to zero.
  Indeed, −£790,000 + £690,000 + £100,000 = 0.

Applications and Benefits

Equity swaps are very popular among hedge funds and other similar institutional organizations as it enables the parties to diversify their cash flows, and hedge or transfer their exposure without having to buy any new shares or assets. There are many other benefits when entering into equity swaps.

First of all, when an investor strategically holds shares in a specific company, they are not only interested in the performance of the company but also in the voting rights they get from their holdings. If this investor believes the company is about to underperform in the short term, they need to hedge their price exposure for a predetermined period of time. They can then sell their shares in the market with the intention to buy them back at a lower price in the future; but they would lose their strategic voting rights on the board. One alternative is to enter into an equity swap where they are the equity leg payer for the same notional of shares they possess. Then they receive an interest payment and have no more price exposure to their shares during the tenor of the swap. As the investor does not sell his shares, they keep their voting rights. At the same time, they avoid the high transaction costs associated with selling/buying a large notional of shares.

Equity swaps are also used to legally get around investment barriers. For example, if a domestic hedge fund wants to be exposed to a foreign security and it cannot invest in it due to strict capital control regulations, it can enter into an equity swap with a resident of the foreign country, where the latter basically buys the shares of the target company and transfers its return against a fixed-income-linked payment. Through, this equity swap, the hedge fund gets the total return of the foreign target company without having to own it. It is important to note that the cash outlay is minimal, even for large notionals. However, this involves significant credit risk exposures. So to minimize this risk, the two swap counterparties may agree to mark-to-market the swap at any point during the life of the transaction. In that case, the remaining time to maturity is segmented into smaller periods and netted payments are performed at the end of each period depending on the equity underlying performance during each time interval.

Next, we consider the example of a private company that strategically owns large stakes in some listed companies. In the event that this private company is looking to acquire stakes in some other listed companies, it may optimize the stake-building process through structured equity derivative solutions by, for instance, delegating the execution and financing of the stake-building to an investment bank through an equity swap.

Figure 3.5 shows how the investment bank (Bank) executes and finances the purchase of shares on behalf of the private company (Client). The bank purchases the shares in the market; the average execution price per share is the "initial price." Simultaneously, Bank and Client enter into an equity swap on the shares purchased by Bank. The equity notional amount is equal to the shares purchase price. Client pays Bank an initial equity investment (a "haircut") such as 25% of the equity notional amount.

The haircut is a percentage that is subtracted from the market value of an asset used as the collateral in a financial operation (a transaction involving securities lending, for example). The haircut could be viewed as the difference between the actual market

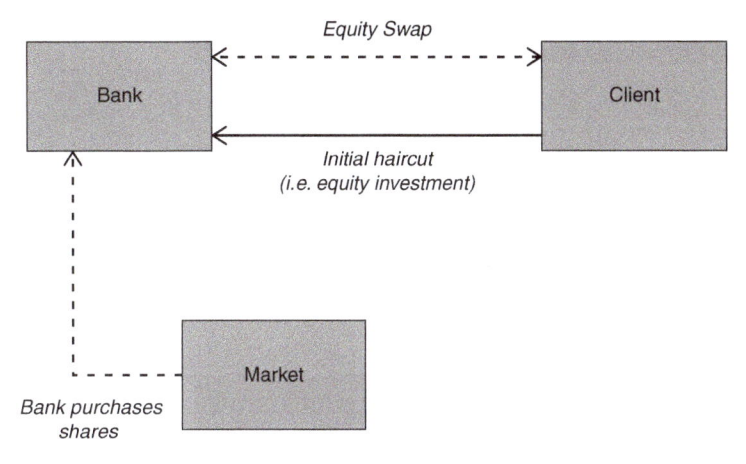

Figure 3.5 Financing and execution of the purchase of shares by a bank on behalf of the client

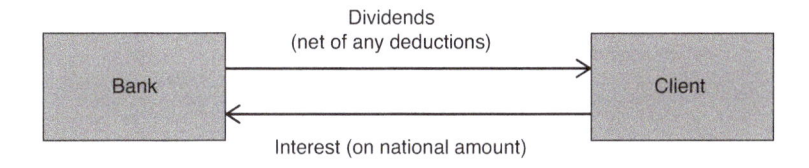

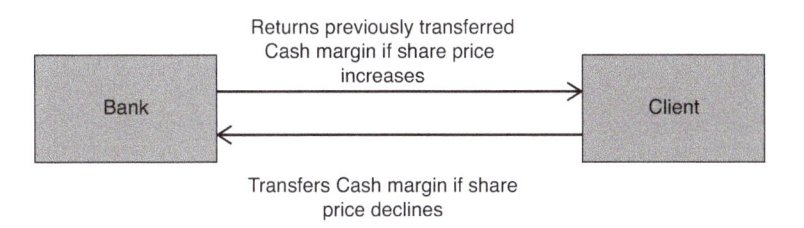

Figure 3.6 Exchanged cash flows during the life of a swap

value of the security used as collateral and the value assessed by the lending side of the transaction. It is then an additional way of mitigating the potential credit risk. The market risk of the collateral and the credit quality of the counterparty are both important factors impacting the percentage of the haircut.

Figure 3.6 gives the cash flows exchanged during the life of the swap. Bank pays Client manufactured dividends (net of any applicable taxes or withholdings) and Client pays Bank a floating-rate interest on a notional amount equal to the original equity notional amount minus the paid haircut, that is, 75% of the equity notional.

Physical Settlement

Bank → Shares delivery → Client

Bank ← Equity National Amount minus Haircut ← Client

Cash Settlement

Bank → Share price appreciation (if any) plus Haircut → Client

Bank ← Share price depreciation (if any) ← Client

⋯⋯⋯→ Bank resells the shares in the market

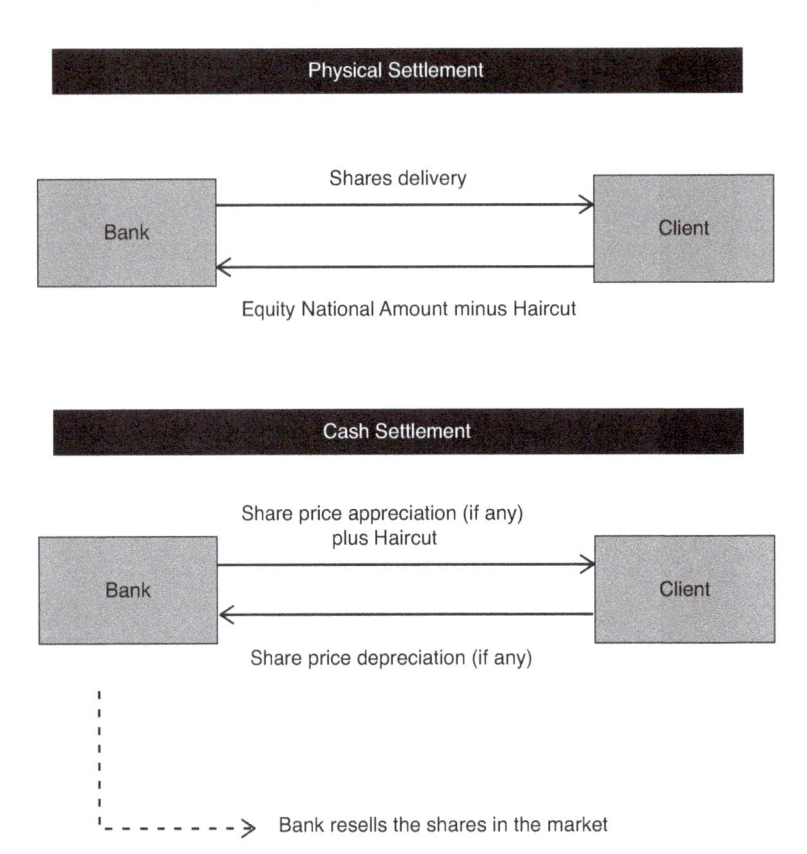

Figure 3.7 Outcomes of an equity swap

amount. The transaction is usually subject to margining, as this enables mitigation of the credit risk.

The client can decide whether they would require actual physical ownership of the shares or whether exposure to the share price would suffice. Figure 3.7 illustrates the outcome under the equity swap depending on the settlement method applicable at maturity. Client may choose physical or cash settlement.

Hedging Equity Swaps

Figure 3.8 shows the hedging process behind most of equity swaps offered by investment banks. When the bank pays the return of Stock X on a notional N, it takes a riskless position by buying the same notional of Stock X for its own trading book from the market. Any equity performance paid or received by the investment bank from the equity swap transaction is offset against the realized P&L from its long position in Stock X. In fact, investment banks do not make their money by speculating on stock markets when dealing equity swaps; their positions are usually hedged, and their P&L comes from commissions, interest spreads and paying lower dividends than the actual amounts received.

Hedging Equity Swaps

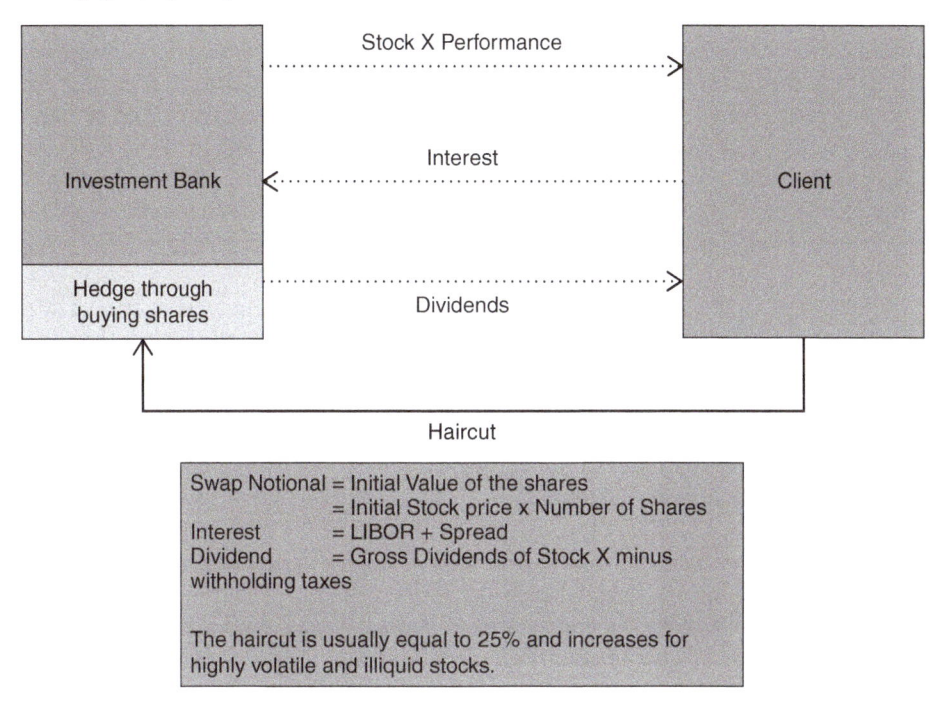

Figure 3.8 Diagram of an equity swap transaction

As it is the case for most plain vanilla swaps, the market value of an equity swap at trade inception is often equal to zero. The pricing concept is similar to that used for traditional interest rates swaps or currency swaps. From each counterparty standpoint, the value of an equity swap is equal to the value of the receiving leg minus the value of the paying leg. At any time during the life of the swap, the value of a fixed-income leg is computed as the net present value of expected future cash flows. On the other hand, equity legs can be valued as discounted expected future dividends plus the present value of a series of forward contracts.

3.4 Dividend Swaps

As mentioned in Chapter 1, dividends represent the percentage of a company's profits that is distributed to shareholders. Dividends may vary depending on how profitable the company is, and they are also heavily impacted by the company's policy in terms of dividend distributions. It is of course very unlikely that an unprofitable company will pay much in the way of dividends to its shareholders. However, it is entirely possible that a company makes profits and decides to reinvest the cash in the development of further projects instead of paying dividends.

As its name implies, a dividend swap is a swap financial instrument and possesses the same payment features as an equity swap. Dividend swaps are also customized OTC derivatives where two counterparties agree to exchange future cash flows at defined intervals over a fixed term (for example annual payments over three years). As with equity swaps, one leg usually involves a fixed-income cash flow that could be based on a fixed or variable interest rate. However, the equity leg is linked to the dividends associated with an equity underlying. The holder of the equity leg receives the realized dividends distributed by a specific stock, or by a basket of stocks or by all the members of an index. Like all vanilla swaps, a swap notional is specified at the initial date.

Like most swaps, dividend swaps are tailored such that their value at issue date is equal to zero. This way, there is no cash exchange between both parties when they enter into the trade. This could be accomplished by making the present value of the fixed-income leg equal to the present value of the expected future dividends associated with the equity underlying. Traded dividend swaps are often used by traders and dealers to estimate a forecast of future dividends to be paid by a specific stock or index during a particular period of time.

Dividend swaps became more and more popular in the early 2000s. During that period, market participants were significantly invested in structured notes and equity-linked notes, so investors gained exposure to the price movements of the underlying security, but not to their dividend streams. Whenever a bank issues a structured note or a derivative financial instrument, traders usually hedge the offer by taking an offsetting position. The payoff from equity derivatives is usually based on the price performance of the underlying only; it does not include dividends features, mostly for tax purposes. Indeed, when a trader takes a short position in a stock forward, the hedge is performed by selling the underlying stock. Then the trader is left holding a stream of future variable dividends that could be more or less volatile. A dividend swap would be useful, as the trader could be short the equity leg to transform these uncertain future payments into fixed payments.

The popularity of the dividend swaps in the early 2000s was because they were considered a great hedge solution against the uncertainty of dividend payments. Now, in the second decade of the 21st century, they are also used as means to play long-term growth strategies by speculating on companies' future dividends. In traditional stock markets, a company's shares are mainly purchased and held in the hope of being sold later at a higher price. Similarly, an investor could enter into a dividend swap being long the equity leg in the hope of increasing their wealth if the underlying company pays out higher dividends than expected. If they have the opposite view of future dividends, they are said to be "short divs" and may invest in a dividend swap as the fixed leg receiver and equity leg payer.

Figure 3.9 shows the mechanism of a typical stock dividend swap. The Fixed Income Amount is equal to the pre-agreed payments; note that these payments could be fixed or variable, as they can be linked to a floating market interest rate such as the LIBOR rate. The Equity Amount represents the sum of qualifying dividends realized during the life of the swap; 100% of the declared dividends are taken into account. The qualifying dividends are usually gross (that is, before tax). At maturity, the payoff of

```
┌─────────────┐         Equity Amount          ┌─────────────┐
│             │<- - - - - - - - - - - - - - - -│             │
│             │       Qualifying Dividends     │             │
│Dividend Buyer│                                │Dividend Seller│
│Equity Leg Receiver│                          │Fixed Leg Receiver│
│             │        Fixed Income Amount     │             │
│             │- - - - - - - - - - - - - - - ->│             │
│             │        Fixed Income payment    │             │
└─────────────┘                                └─────────────┘
```

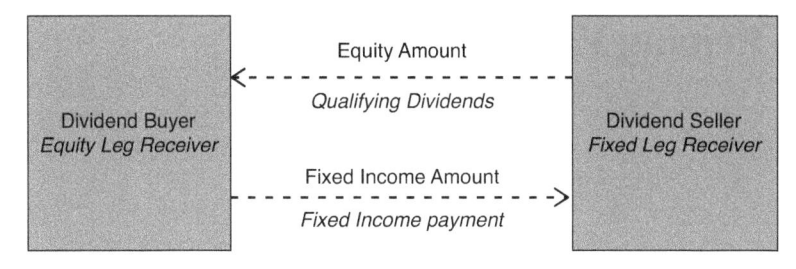

Figure 3.9 Dividend swaps mechanism

the dividend buyer is equal to:

$$\text{Payoff}_{\text{Dividend Buyer}} = \text{Number of Shares}$$
$$\times \{\text{Equity Amount} - \text{Fixed Income Amount}\}$$

Investing in dividend swaps is a zero-sum game; the profit of the first counterparty is equal to the loss of the other counterparty. Then the payoff of the dividend seller is as follows:

$$\text{Payoff}_{\text{Dividend Seller}} = \text{Number of Shares}$$
$$\times \{\text{Fixed Income Amount} - \text{Equity Amount}\}$$

Dividend swaps have proved to be good investments during the period 2000–2010. At first, banks created dividend swaps to offset dividend risks. The main players were proprietary desks and some hedge funds. Thanks to more standardized confirmations, the liquidity of dividend swaps has increased significantly. There is a low correlation between dividends and other asset classes. Dividend swaps not only provide portfolio diversification but can also provide protection against market volatility.

During periods when stock markets become very nervous and volatility increases significantly, dividends are still quite stable, so entering into dividend swaps enables investors to receive a stable income stream.

4 Pricing Vanilla Options

4.1 European Calls and Puts

European equity options are financial instruments that provide the holder with the right, but not the obligation, to buy or sell an equity underlying at a pre-agreed price (the strike price) on a specified future date, the maturity date. It is the choice of the holder of the option to exercise their right to buy/sell the underlying at the strike price. The term "European" means that the exercise date may only take place on the option expiry date. European options can be standardized and exchange-traded or negotiated over the counter. The equity underlying could be a stock, a basket of stocks or a stock market index. Again, one can choose between physical and cash delivery at the inception of trade. Today, European options are widely traded by most market players, who are so used to their payoff mechanism that they call them vanilla financial products.

The call option gives the holder the right to buy the equity underlying, whereas the put option gives the buyer the right to sell it. At any point of time t, if the strike price K is equal to the stock price S_t, the European option is said to be at-the-money spot (ATM Spot). If the strike is equal to the theoretical forward price on option maturity, the call or put option is defined as at-the-money forward (ATM Forward). Figure 4.1 indicates whether an option is said to be out-of-the-money (OTM) or in-the-money (ITM), depending on whether the strike price is greater or lower than the spot price. If we compute an option payoff as if it were due today and the payoff is found to be strictly positive, the option is ITM. If it is strictly negative, the option is said to be OTM.

Let n be the number of shares to be bought as specified in the call option contract and S_T be the underlying stock price at maturity. The payoff to the holder of a single stock call option is as follows:

$$Payoff_{Call} = n \times Max\{0, S_T - K\}$$

In practice, option prices are negotiated in terms of percentage of the notional N. Accordingly, the strike price is expressed as a percentage of the initial spot price S_0. If we readjust the above payoff formula, we get:

$$Payoff_{Call} = n \times S_0 \times Max\left\{0, \frac{S_T - K}{S_0}\right\}$$

Then

$$Payoff_{Call} = N \times Max\left\{0, Perf_T - \frac{K}{S_0}\right\}$$

Where $N = n \times S_0$ and $Perf_T = \frac{S_T}{S_0}$.

Option Type	Strike vs Spot	Moneyness
Call Option	S > K	ITM
Call Option	S = K	ATM
Call Option	S < K	OTM
Put Option	S > K	OTM
Put Option	S = K	ATM
Put Option	S < K	ITM

Figure 4.1 Moneyness of European call and put options

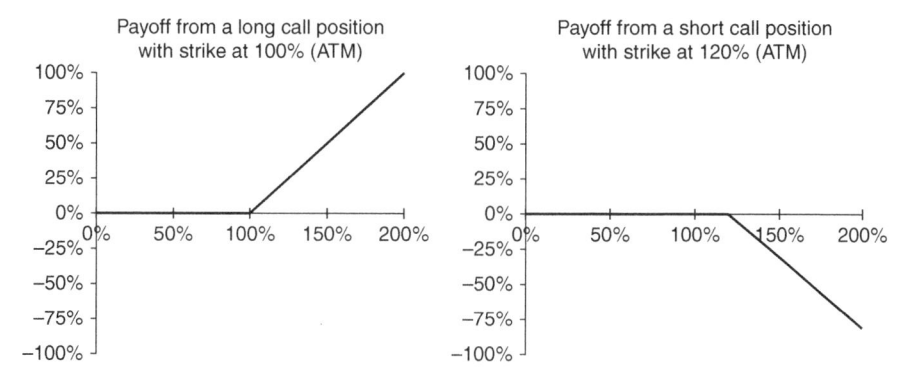

Figure 4.2 Payoff of a long ATM call position and payoff of a short OTM call position

Here, we can note that the payoff of a call option is asymmetric, as it can only be positive; the maximum loss for a call option holder is the premium they pay at inception date to buy this derivative. The potential payoff of a European call can be infinite. Figure 4.2 shows payoff graphs of buyers and sellers of European call options. Payoffs are expressed in percentage of notional depending on the stock's performance $\frac{S_T}{S_0}$. On the left-hand side, the graph indicates the payoff to be paid to the buyer of an at-the-money call option. The payoff on the right-hand side is derived from a short position in a call with a strike at 120%, i.e. $\frac{K}{S_0} = 120\%$.

The holder of a call option will only exercise their option if the underlying stock's market price at maturity is higher than the strike price. This way, their payoff is positive and equal to $N \times (Perf_T - K)$ as they buy the underlying stock at a price K lower than the market price. Here K is expressed in percentage of the initial spot price. Note that the profit from holding a call option is equal to the payoff at maturity less the premium paid at inception. Clients can buy call options to speculate on the price of a specific stock. If they believe the underlying stock's price will increase above the specified strike price at the expiry date, they will buy a European call. But if an investor has a bearish view of the underlying stock's price, they will sell a European call option, to get a premium price. Then their gain (if any) is locked to the premium, whereas their maximum loss is unlimited. Investors usually take the risk of selling options in order to get extra income if their prognosis proves correct.

Other clients may be willing to acquire a specific number of shares from an underlying company at a future date. Buying call options enables them to hedge against a rising price of the underlying stock. If the stock price increases in the future, the call option holder is completely hedged as they can exercise their option and buy the company shares at the strike price; and if the price of the underlying drops, the option holder would leave it to expire unexercised and could still buy the stocks at a lower price. Call options provide some kind of insurance against the increase of an underlying stock price while still benefiting from a downside in the market price. This insurance attracts a price, and this price is called the premium.

Figure 4.3 shows the profit graphs from two independent long positions in a one-year forward contract and a European call option with the same strike and the same maturity date. The initial spot price is equal to $70 and both contracts are written on 20,000 shares. The notional N is then equal to $1,400,000. The strike price is equal to 110% of the initial spot price: $77. We assume the long position in the forward contract was taken at zero cost, as the strike price was equal to the theoretical forward price at the trade inception date. Let's also assume that the holder of the call option had to pay a premium priced at 7% of the notional. The long forward position makes a profit if the spot price at maturity is higher than 110% of the initial spot price. However, it can suffer a maximum loss equal to the number of shares times the strike price. The call option holder makes a profit if the underlying price at maturity is greater than $110\% + 7\% = 117\%$ of the initial spot price. However, its maximum loss is capped at 7%.

Let's take the example of the two positions in Figure 4.3. If we assume the underlying's market price at maturity S_T is equal to 93% of the initial spot price S_0 (that is, $65.10), then the payoff from the call option would be equal to $1,400,000 × Max $\{0, 93\% - 110\%\} = \$0$. The total loss from buying the call option would be equal to $1,400,000 × 7% = $98,000. The long forward position would have to pay to the

Profits from bullish positions

——— Profit from buying a European call option
- - - Profit from a long forward position

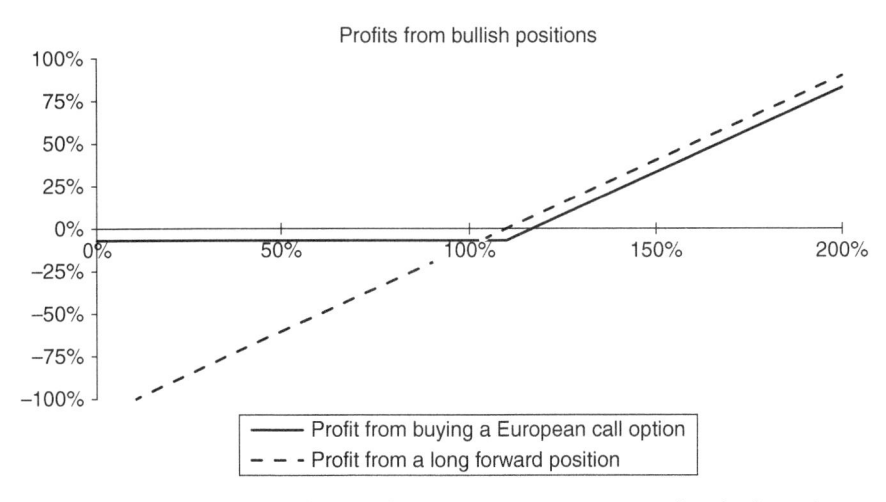

Figure 4.3 Comparison of profits from long positions in a European call and a forward contract with identical strikes at 110%

short forward position an amount equal to $1,400,000 \times (110\% - 93\%) = \$238,000$. In this downside scenario, it's clear that the loss from being long a forward contract is greater than the loss from buying a call option. Now, assuming $S_T = 115\%$, the payoff from the long call position is equal to $1,400,000 \times Max\{0, 115\% - 110\%\} = \$70,000$. And since the call premium is equal to $1,400,000 \times 7\% = \$98,000$, then the P&L of the long call position is negative and equal to $\$70,000 - \$98,000 = \$-28,000$. On the other hand, the long forward position makes a profit of $1,400,000 \times (115\% - 110\%) = \$70,000$.

As previously mentioned, European put options provide their holder with the right to sell a specific quantity n of an equity underlying at the strike price K on the maturity date T. Their payoff is as follows:

$$Payoff_{Put} = n \times Max\{0, K - S_T\}$$

or

$$Payoff_{Put} = N \times Max\left\{0, \frac{K}{S_0} - Perf_T\right\}$$

where n is the number of shares and N is the contract notional.

Like call options, payoffs of put options are asymmetric; they can only be positive. That is why buyers of put options need to pay a positive premium; to get the right to lock a selling price. The maximum loss for a put option holder is the premium they pay at the inception of the trade. The maximum payoff of a European put is not infinite and is capped at $N \times \frac{K}{S_0}$ or $n \times K$ (if the stock price becomes null). Figure 4.4 shows the payoff at maturity of long and short positions in European put options. As is the case in Figure 4.4, payoffs are expressed in percentage of notional depending on the performance of the underlying stock $\frac{S_T}{S_0}$. On the left-hand side, the graph indicates the payoff to be received by the buyer of an at-the-money put option. On the right, the payoff is that of a short position in an in-the-money European put with a strike at 130%, i.e. $\frac{K}{S_0} = 130\%$.

A European put option will only be exercised by its holder in the case where the price of the underlying stock at maturity is lower than its strike price. Exercising a European put is equivalent to selling the underlying stock at a price higher than the market price at maturity. The profit from holding a European put option is equal to

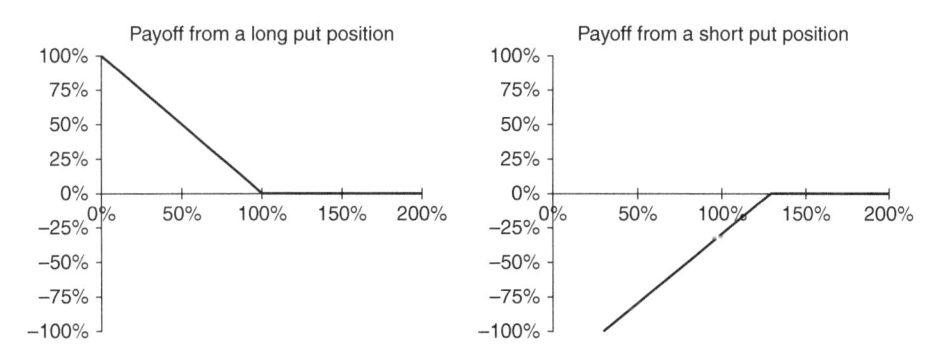

Figure 4.4 Payoff of a long position in a European put with strike at 100% and from a short position in a European put with strike at 110%

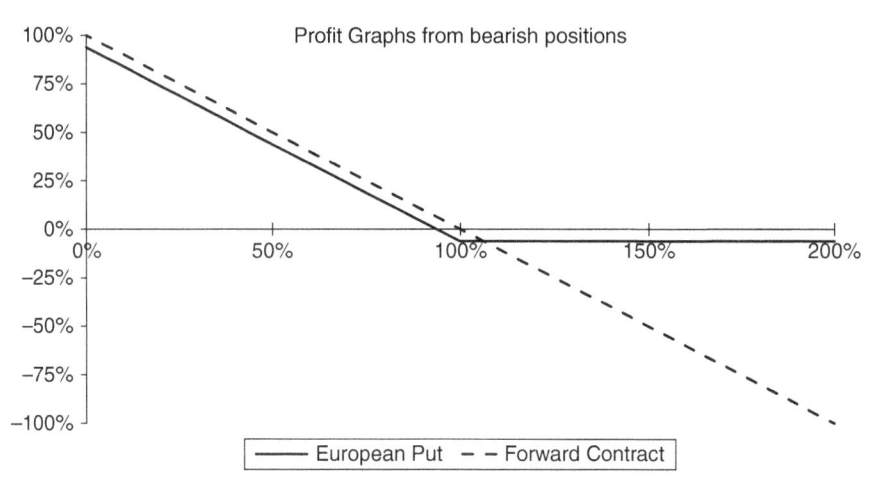

Figure 4.5 Comparison of profits from long positions in a European put and a forward contract with identical strikes

the payoff at maturity less the premium paid at inception. Put options can be used as means of speculating on a drop in the underlying stock price; an investor would sell a European put to earn a premium price if they have a bullish view of the price of the underlying stock. Speculators usually take the risk of selling options in order to get extra income if their hoped-for scenario is realized.

Apart from speculators, there exist a wide range of clients that use put options to hedge against a potentially decreasing price of a specific underlying stock. For example, there could be clients willing to sell a quantity of an underlying equity security in, say, three months' time. Buying a three-month European put option would enable them to cap the selling price to the strike price in three months' time. On the maturity date, if the stock price finishes below the strike price, the put is exercised and the stock sold at K (a price higher than the market price). Otherwise, the option is not used and the holder can still sell the underlying stock at the market price.

Figure 4.5 shows the profits from two independent bearish positions written on the same underlying stock with the same maturity date: a short position in a forward contract and a long position in a European put option bought at 6% premium. Let's assume $S_0 = \$85$ and $n = 120,000$; then the notional N is equal to $\$10,200,000$. From the graph, we can observe that the strike price for both contracts is identical and equal to 100% of the initial spot price. We can also consider the case of a zero-cost forward contract; the forward contract has been initially priced such that its present value is null; neither of the counterparties has to pay a single cent to enter into the forward. The short forward position makes a profit if S_T is lower than 100% of the initial spot price, but loses uncapped sums of money in a rising price environment. The holder of the at-the-money put option makes a positive P&L if the underlying's price at maturity is lower than $100\% - 6\% = 94\%$. As for all option holders, its maximum loss is capped at the premium of 6%, whereas the maximum loss for a short forward position can be infinite.

Buyer	Counterparty L
Seller	Counterparty S
UnderlyingAsset	Unilever
Number of Shares	125 000
Currency	GBP
Initial Spot Price	28, 62
Strike Price	27, 50
Initial Date	May 24, 2013
Maturity Date	May 25, 2015
Settlement Date	May 27, 2015
Premium	GBP 339,865

Figure 4.6 Terms of a two-year European put option

EXERCISE

In Figure 4.6 we can see the termsheet of an OTC European put contract involving Counterparty L and Counterparty S respectively as the buyer and the seller of the two-year put option. If the market price on May 25, 2015 of one Unilever share is equal to £22.30, what would be the P&L for both counterparts?

Discussion

Profit and Loss for Counterparty L:
Counterparty L is the put option buyer. At the trade date, he pays a premium of £339,865 to Counterparty S. The payoff Counterparty L receives on May 27, 2015 is equal to 125,000 Max{0, 27.50 − 22.30} = £650,000.
Counterparty L makes an overall profit equal to £650,000 − £339,865 = £310,135.

Profit and Loss for Counterparty S:
Counterparty S is the short counterparty. At the trade date, he receives a premium of £339,865 from Counterparty L to sell the two-year European put option. Based on the observed price of £22.30 on the maturity date, Counterparty S must pay a payoff amount of £650,000 (calculation details as per above) on the settlement date.
The P&L for Counterparty S is then equal to £339,865 − £650,000 = −£310,135.

4.2 Hedging Cost Principle

In this chapter, we focus on what is probably the most important concept in pricing and trading: the hedging cost principle. Fully understanding this concept enables the practitioner to acquire the mindset of a successful trader; so a full section is devoted to explaining the concept clearly. In finance, a trader is seen as successful if on average they buy low and sell high, thus making a profit for their organization. As previously explained, most practitioners on trading floors do not offer financial products to their clients without hedging them. Apart from speculators, traders do not gamble with the money of the shareholders; they do not usually take naked positions, and they do create an offsetting position whenever they issue a new derivative. On looking at a trader's book or portfolio, it will be seen that the overall market exposure lies within predetermined limits.

Again, it is very important to understand this hedging concept. Basically, when one sells a derivative A with a payoff $Payoff_A$, hedging this position means buying another product B with payoff $Payoff_B$ such that $Payoff_A = Payoff_B$. Therefore the aggregate position {Sell A and Buy B} has zero exposure to the market, as the overall payoff at maturity is equal to $-Payoff_B + Payoff_A = 0$. The trader makes profit by offering the derivative A at a price slightly higher than the hedge B. In this example, the hedge is full and static; this means the trader only needs to buy one single product B at the inception of the trade to replicate the payoff of the issued product A.

The hedging process depends on the type of offered derivatives. For exotic and sophisticated products, the offsetting position can sometimes be very difficult to achieve. A model is then used to represent the evolution of the different market parameters that impact the price of the issued derivative. The trader tries to model the performance of interest rates, the dividends, the price of the underlying and its volatility from the proposed inception date up to the maturity of the trade. The idea is to create a dynamic offsetting position by buying and selling variable quantities of the equity underlying and other financial products on a periodic basis. This dynamic hedge is achieved using the measures of risk obtained from the model that has been used.

A dynamic hedge is always much more time-consuming and complicated than a static hedge. However, it is necessary when it comes to cover a position involving a more or less complicated derivative. Yes, the hedge is not perfect, as it is obtained from a model and models are not perfect by construction; indeed, there have been many cases where a financial institution lost money because some of the models used were not correct; i.e. the behavior of the underlying security in the real world proved to be different from the modeled behavior. This could create a loss for the institution if the offsetting position costs more than the profit from the issued position. However, investing in model research and mastering complicated products offers banks a great competitive edge that opens the way to potentially large and lucrative markets.

A good hedge is a hedge whose payoff of the issued position is equal to the payoff of the offsetting position no matter how the market evolves during the life of the trade. This way, the portfolio risk is under strong control, and the profit comes from the trading fees that increase as the volumes exchanged increase. When a client is willing to enter into a specific derivative position and asks banks for quotes, the traders of these financial institutions will look for a way to hedge that particular derivative. Obviously, depending on their risk limits and their view on the market, they may decide to fully or partially hedge some aspects and parameters of the trade. Once the offsetting position has been defined, the traders need to quote a price to their clients, and this is the critical point: What should this price be in order to be competitive and not lose money in the hedging process? First, the minimal price (the theoretical one) should be equal to the cost of hedging the position. Then each trader adds discretionary fees.

Now that it is clear that the price of any derivative is equal to the cost of hedge, it is possible for a trader to price vanilla and exotic products as long as they know how to hedge it. This is a much more efficient and reliable way to look at trading. The cost of hedge principle is, again, a critical concept in the world of derivatives, as it creates a bridge between theory and practice. There is no need to learn reams of pricing formulas by heart. And even if a trader were willing to forgo the intellectual beauty of thinking, it would still not be enough to learn pricing formulas alone. Indeed, new financial derivatives will appear to respond to the needs of evolving markets and economies. And a successful trader must be able to offer these products; that is, to price an offer realistically after taking the hedging process into account and estimating the associated cost.

4.3 Pricing Vanillas

The idea behind pricing any type of derivative is to model the movement of the price of the underlying equity so that it follows the market's behavior as closely as possible. Once we have the right model, the payoff at maturity can be estimated and we derive an implied price from this payoff. To evaluate European options, most market players use the Black–Scholes (or Black–Scholes–Merton) formula, derived from a mathematical model articulated by Fisher Black and Myron Scholes in 1973. This pricing formula has been widely used as it has been empirically proven that market prices for European-style options follow the Black–Scholes theoretical prices closely. This model assumes that the underlying stock price follows a log-normal distribution; that is, that the return of the stock price follows a normal distribution.

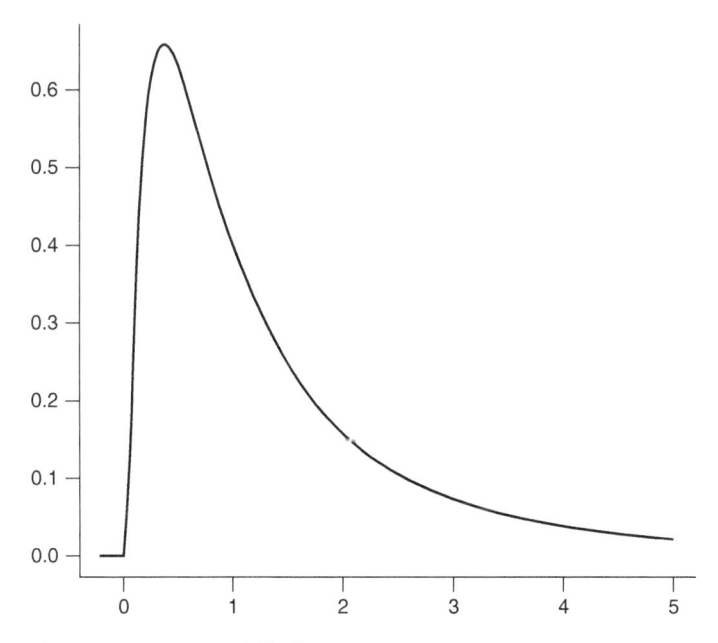

Figure 4.7 Log-normal distribution

Here, it is interesting to note that several assumptions under Black–Scholes model are far from realistic. For example, the model assumes the lending rate r is constant and equal to the borrowing rate, that the transaction costs and fees are null, and so on. Even if some of these assumptions are not verified in the market, it is still the predominant pricing formula in the market, for at least two reasons. First, it is a closed formula, which implies that the calculation is easily, almost quickly, performed. Second and most important, the fact that everybody uses this formula to quote options in the market makes it by construction a good model. Let $Call_{BS}(t)$ be the Black–Scholes price at time T for a European-style call option with maturity T and strike K:

$$Call_{BS}(t) = S_t \times e^{-q \times (T-t)} \times N(d_1) - K \times e^{-r \times (T-t)} \times N(d_2)$$

with

$$d_1 = \frac{\ln\left(\frac{S_t}{K}\right) + \left(r - q + \frac{\sigma^2}{2}\right)(T-t)}{\sigma \sqrt{T-t}}$$

$$d_2 = d_1 - \sigma \sqrt{T-t}$$

And $N(x)$ is the cumulative probability up to the standardized normal value x:

$$N(x) = P(X < x) = \int_{-\infty}^{x} \frac{1}{\sqrt{2\Pi}} e^{-\frac{1}{2}x^2} dx$$

The shaded area in Figure 4.8 is equal to $N(z)$. As the graph is symmetrical around 0, then we can see that the white area is equal to $N(-z)$. The total area under the graph being equal to 1, then $N(-z) + N(z) = 1$ or $N(-z) = 1 - N(z)$.

$$Put_{BS}(t) = K \times e^{-r \times (T-t)} \times N(-d_2) - S_t \times e^{-q \times (T-t)} \times N(-d_1)$$

or

$$Put_{BS}(t) = S_t \times e^{-q \times (T-t)} \times (N(d_1) - 1) - K \times e^{-r \times (T-t)} \times (N(d_2) - 1)$$

Figures 4.9 and 4.10 represent the theoretical prices of European calls and puts. The price curves are compared to the payoff graphs and emphasize the fact that the option prices are most often higher than their payoffs. As time approaches maturity date, the

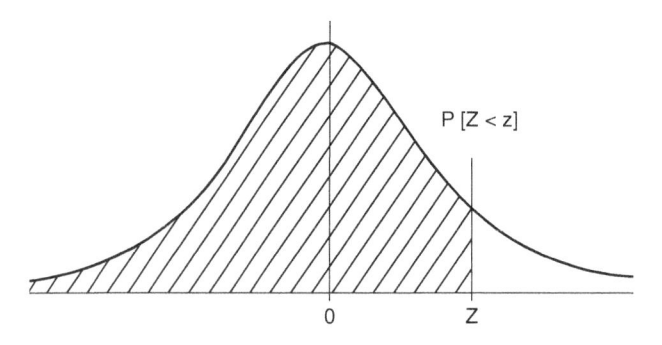

Figure 4.8 Cumulative probability up to the standardized normal value

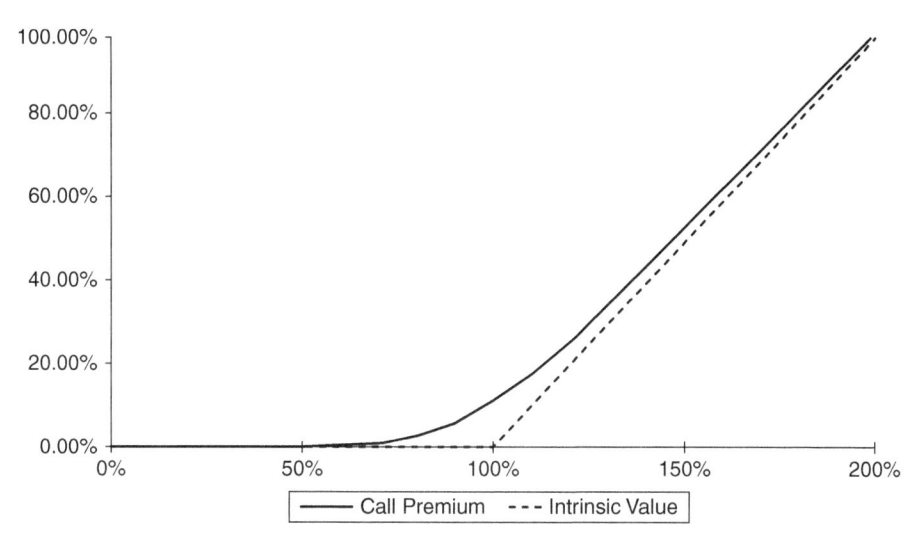

Figure 4.9 Price of a one-year European call struck at 100% with respect to the underlying spot price

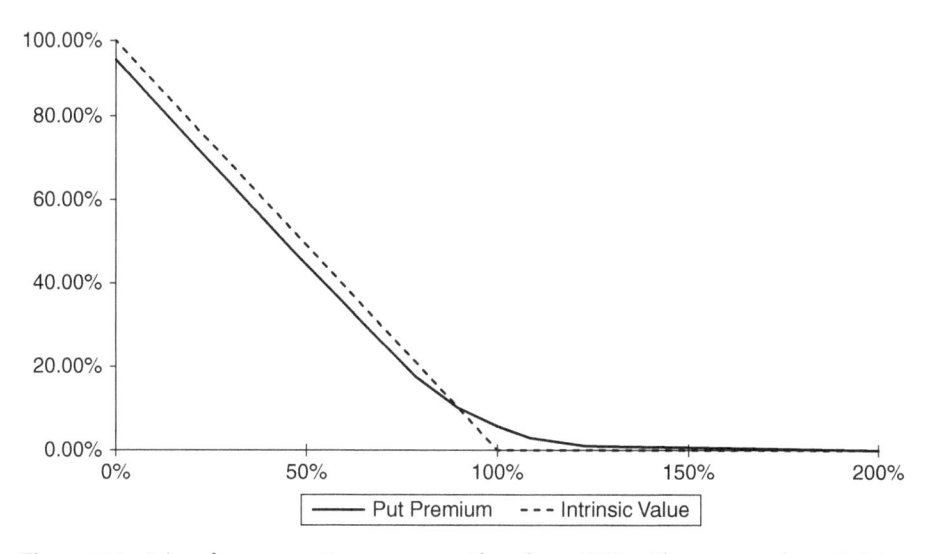

Figure 4.10 Price of a one-year European put with strike at 100% with respect to the underlying spot price

value of options moves towards the payoff. In the case of in-the-money European put options, the premium may be greater than the intrinsic value. We explain this situation in detail when we discuss Theta in Chapter 5. At expiry date, the price of an option is equal to the payoff value. The market price of an option could be segmented into its intrinsic value plus its time value. An option's intrinsic value at time t is equal to its payoff if it were to be exercised at t. It is positive when the option is in-the-money, and null otherwise.

$$\text{Intrinsic Value}_{\text{Call}}(t) = \text{Max}\{0; S_t - K\}$$
$$\text{Intrinsic Value}_{\text{Put}}(t) = \text{Max}\{0; K - S_t\}$$

The difference between the option price and the intrinsic value is equal to the time value. From Figures 4.9 and 4.10, we can see that the time value is almost null when an option is deep-in-the-money and deep-out-of-the-money. Moreover, the time value is maximal when the option is at-the-money. The time value becomes higher as maturity gets longer and volatility is higher. The time value decreases as time to maturity decreases, and becomes null at maturity. Therefore, the price of a call option with strike K and maturity T_2 is greater than the price of the same option written on the same underlying with the same strike and a lower maturity, T_1.

Call-put parity

Now to prove one very important result, commonly known as the "call-put parity." To do this, consider two strategies, A and B.

Portfolio A:
- Long a European call on Stock X with maturity T and strike K.
- Short a European put written on the same stock with maturity T and strike K.

Portfolio B:
- Long a forward contract on Stock X with maturity T and strike K.

Evaluate the respective payoffs at maturity Payoff$_A$ and Payoff$_B$ of portfolios A and B:

Scenario 1: $S_T \geq K$
Payoff$_A$ = Max$\{0, S_T - K\}$ − Max$\{0, K - S_T\}$
Payoff$_A$ = $S_T - K - 0$
Payoff$_A$ = $S_T - K$

and

Payoff$_B$ = $S_T - K$
=> Payoff$_A$ = Payoff$_B$ under Scenario 1

Scenario 2: $S_T < K$
Payoff$_A$ = Max$\{0, S_T - K\}$ − Max$\{0, K - S_T\}$
Payoff$_A$ = $0 - (K - S_T)$
Payoff$_A$ = $S_T - K$

and

Payoff$_B$ = $S_T - K$
=> Payoff$_A$ = Payoff$_B$ under Scenario 2

Under all scenarios, both portfolios have the same payoff. Therefore, the value of Portfolio A is equal to the value of Portfolio B at any point of time t; which means:

$$\text{Call}(t) - \text{Put}(t) = \text{Forward}_{\text{long}}(t)$$

which leads to the call/put parity:

$$\text{Call}(t) - \text{Put}(t) = S_t \times e^{-q \times (T-t)} - K \times e^{-r \times (T-t)}$$

If we look closely at this formula, we can see that we can create synthetic vanilla derivatives by combining other equity derivatives. This could be very useful if, for example, a specific call option is not available on the market. One could then create a synthetic call by combining puts and forwards on the same underlying with the same maturity and strike. The call/put parity leads to the following relationships:

- Synthetic long position in a forward contract: Long a call and short a put.
- Synthetic short position in a forward contract: Short a call and long a put.
- Long a synthetic call option: Long a put option and long a forward contract.
- Long a synthetic put: Long a call option and short a forward contract.

Note that these relationships could be easily proved by adding the payoffs of the different positions' combinations and showing that it is equal to the payoff of the synthetic derivative position.

4.4 American Options

The following defines American options in a basic way: American options are derivative instruments that provide the holder with the right, but not the obligation, to buy or sell an underlying equity asset at a predefined strike price K. The main distinction compared with European options is the exercise process; American options can be exercised at any time up to and including the expiry date, whereas European options can only be exercised at maturity date T. American calls are the options to buy the underlying stock, and American puts are options to sell it. As it is the case for most options, the underlying equity asset could be a single stock, a basket of stocks, or an index.

American and European options are not related to the United States or Europe. Bermudan options are another type of options with a similar payoff to American and European payoffs, but differing from those in the exercise period. Indeed, Bermudan options are exercisable at maturity date and also on predetermined dates that occur between the initial date and the expiration date – exercise dates typically occur on a monthly basis.

The payoff of American calls and puts written on n stocks are as follows:

$$\text{Payoff}_{\text{American Call}} = n \times \text{Max}\{0, S_t - K\}$$
$$\text{Payoff}_{\text{American Put}} = n \times \text{Max}\{0, K - S_t\}$$

Here, S_t is the underlying stock's market price at the chosen exercise date. American options work in the same way as European options, but give more flexibility to the holder, who can exercise them at any time during the life of the options. Let $\text{Price}_{\text{EC}}(t)$ and $\text{Price}_{\text{EP}}(t)$ be the respective theoretical values at time t of European calls and puts written on Stock X with maturity T and strike K. Also let $\text{Price}_{\text{AC}}(t)$ and $\text{Price}_{\text{AP}}(t)$ be the respective theoretical values at time t of American calls and puts written on the same underlying stock with the same maturity and strike. Since American options provide their holder with more optionality, then it is quite easy to understand that their price will be higher or at least equal to the price of European options with the same features:

$$\text{Price}_{EC}(t) \leq \text{Price}_{AC}(t)$$

and

$$\text{Price}_{EP}(t) \leq \text{Price}_{AP}(t)$$

There is no Black–Scholes or any other closed formula to easily price American options. However, there are multiple models to approximate their value. Among the list of available pricing methods for American options, Monte Carlo simulations, Whaley or binomial options models may be used. At any point of time t during the life of the American option, its holder has the choice between exercising it and selling the option on the market. Remember that the price of an option could be viewed as the sum of its intrinsic value and its time value; exercising the American option implies being paid its intrinsic value, whereas selling it means receiving its market price: the intrinsic value plus the time value. So why might an American option holder be willing to exercise their option instead of selling it? In other words, what would be the extra benefit of buying an American option compared to a European option?

The mathematical and theoretical answer is quite obvious: If the time value at time t is positive, then selling the option is the wiser choice. Otherwise, exercising it is worth more. Most often, American options are not exercised early, as they usually have a non-negative time value. This logic applies in a liquid market for American options where the market price is close to the theoretical price. Indeed, imagine you wish to sell an illiquid American option and you cannot find a buyer in the market, then you cannot sell your option. And being able to exercise your American option becomes very valuable if you need cash and your option is in-the-money.

Now, let's assume we are trading in a liquid market. What would be the optimal time to exercise an American call or put option? To answer this question, we use one fundamental theory based on the absence of arbitrage opportunity. In other words, if Portfolio A gives more profit than Portfolio B, then the value of Portfolio A is greater than the value of Portfolio B. First of all, let's look at the case of American call options. Let EuroCall$_X$ and AmCall$_X$ be respectively European and American call options written on the underlying stock X with maturity date T and strike price K. Let Q be the future value at time T of the dividends distributed by Stock X during the life of the options. Eventually let S_t be the market price of Stock X at time t. Now let's define strategies A and B at time t as follows:

Portfolio A: Purchase Stock X at price S_t
Portfolio B: Purchase EuroCall$_X$ and make a deposit equal to $(Q+K) \times e^{-r \times (T-t)}$
Let Value$_A(t)$ and Value$_B(t)$ be the respective values of Portfolio A and Portfolio B at any point in time t:

$$\text{Value}_A(t) = S_t$$

and

$$\text{Value}_B(t) = \text{Price}_{EC}(t) + Q \times e^{-r \times (T-t)} + K \times e^{-r \times (T-t)}$$

Evaluate the respective payoffs at maturity $Payoff_A$ and $Payoff_B$ of portfolios A and B:

Scenario 1: $S_T \geq K$
$Payoff_A = S_T + Q$
$Payoff_B = Max\{0, S_T - K\} + Q + K$
$Payoff_B = S_T - K + Q + K$
$Payoff_B = S_T + Q$
$\quad \Rightarrow Payoff_A = Payoff_B$ under scenario 1

Scenario 2: $S_T < K$
$Payoff_A = S_T + Q$
$Payoff_B = Max\{0, S_T - K\} + Q + K$
$Payoff_B = 0 + Q + K$
$Payoff_B = K + Q$

And since $S_T < K$
$\quad \Rightarrow Payoff_A < Payoff_B$ under scenario 2

Here, we conclude that $Payoff_A \leq Payoff_B$ in all cases. It follows that at any time t, the value or price of Portfolio A must be lower than that of Portfolio B.

$$Value_A(t) \leq Value_B(t)$$

Then

$$S_t \leq Price_{EC}(t) + Q \times e^{-r \times (T-t)} + K \times e^{-r \times (T-t)}$$

Moreover, $Price_{EC}(t) \leq Price_{AC}(t)$
We get $S_t \leq Price_{AC}(t) + Q \times e^{-r \times (T-t)} + K \times e^{-r \times (T-t)}$

$$\Rightarrow Price_{AC}(t) \geq S_t - Q \times e^{-r \times (T-t)} - K \times e^{-r \times (T-t)}$$

An American option would be exercised if it is in-the-money and its price is lower or equal to its intrinsic value, i.e. in the case where

$$S_t - K \geq Price_{AC}(t)$$

$$S_t - K \geq S_t - Q \times e^{-r \times (T-t)} - K \times e^{-r \times (T-t)} \Leftrightarrow \frac{Q}{K} \geq 1 - e^{-r \times (T-t)}$$

In other words, there would exist an optimal time t where it would be worth more to exercise the American option earlier if the following relation is verified:
$\frac{Q}{K} \geq 1 - e^{-r \times (T-t)}$

We can simplify $1 - e^{-r \times (T-t)}$ by $r(T - t)$ using a first-order approximation. It follows that it would be optimal to exercise the American call option at time t before the expiry date if

$$\frac{Q}{K} \geq r(T - t)$$

Assuming you have bought the American call option, Q/K could be viewed as a dividend yield you are entitled to if you exercise the option and hold the stocks bought. Keep in mind that exercising the option implies paying an amount of cash equal to the strike price K to acquire the underlying stock. $r(T-t)$ represents the interest rate you receive up to the expiry date on the cash amount K if the option is not exercised early at time t. An intuitive way of understanding the logic behind the above formula could be as follows. It would be optimal to exercise the American call option at time t if the dividend yield from acquiring the underlying stocks is greater than the cash deposit rate. Here it is important to note that it is never optimal to exercise American call options written on non-dividend-paying shares.

Similarly, we can prove that it is optimal to exercise American put options at time t and sell the shares at strike K if the deposit rate is greater than the dividend yield up to the maturity date. And more specifically, it is always better to exercise an American put option when the underlying share pays no dividends provided it is deep in-the-money.

4.5 Asian Options

Asian options are options that have a payoff depending on the average price of the equity underlying computed through the life of the option. Asian options are fairly similar to European options in that there is only one exercise date, the maturity date. However, the payoff is path-dependent. Indeed, all the closing prices of the underlying stock from the initial date up to the expiry date are needed to compute the payoff of Asian options. For European options, the behavior of the underlying share's price during the life of the option is not taken into account – it is only the price at maturity that is important. The payoffs of Asian calls and puts written on a quantity n of underlying stocks are as follows:

- For an Asian call with averaging on the price:

$$\text{Payoff}_{\text{AsianCall}} = n \times \text{Max}\{0, S_{\text{average}} - K\}$$

- For an Asian put with averaging on the price:

$$\text{Payoff}_{\text{AsianPut}} = n \times \text{Max}\{0, K - S_{\text{average}}\}$$

The price of European and Asian options gets higher as volatility increases. Compared to European options, the payoff of Asian options becomes less uncertain as time goes by. For example, a stock could exhibit stable prices during a period of one year and there could one single extraordinary event during the expiry date that completely changes the expected payoff. But in the case of Asian options, this single event would have a very low impact on the final payoff, as the full path of stock prices is taken into account. This implied decrease in volatility makes the Asian options cheaper than European options with the same characteristics. If the maturity is very long, then there could be a significant price difference between Asian and European options. All things being equal, the expected payoff from a European option is then higher than that of an Asian option with the same features.

Moreover, there exists another type of Asian option where the averaging is performed on the strike price; i.e. $K = S_{\text{average}}$ in the payoff of a European call. This means that the buying price (in the case of a call) and the selling price (in the case of a put) are determined as the average of the underlying price during a full period. Their payoffs are the following:

- For an Asian call with averaging on the strike:

$$\text{Payoff}_{\text{AsianCall}} = n \times \text{Max}\{0, S_T - S_{\text{average}}\}$$

- For an Asian put with averaging on the strike:

$$\text{Payoff}_{\text{AsianPut}} = n \times \text{Max}\{0, S_{\text{average}} - S_T\}$$

In the payoff formulas above, S_{average} is the average price of the underlying stock from the initial date up to the maturity date. The average could be arithmetic or geometric. The most convenient and intuitive way for clients is obviously the arithmetic average. Pricewise, the arithmetic sum of log-normal variables (price of the underlying share) does not have good analytical properties. However the geometric sum of log-normal variables follows a log-normal distribution. Therefore it becomes possible to find a closed formula to price Asian options with arithmetic averaging on the price. The Black–Scholes pricing formulas have been readapted and lead to:

$$\text{AsianCall}_{\text{BS}}(t) = S_t \times e^{-q' \times (T-t)} \times N(d_1) - K \times e^{-r \times (T-t)} \times N(d_2)$$

and

$$\text{AsianPut}_{\text{BS}}(t) = K \times e^{-r \times (T-t)} \times N(-d_2) - S_t \times e^{-q' \times (T-t)} \times N(-d_1)$$

with

$$d_1 = \frac{\ln\left(\frac{S_t}{K}\right) + \left(r - q' + \frac{(\sigma')^2}{2}\right) \times (T-t)}{\sigma' \sqrt{T-t}}$$

$$d_2 = d_1 - \sigma' \sqrt{T-t}$$

$$\sigma' = \frac{\sigma}{3}$$

$$q' = \frac{r + q + \frac{\sigma^2}{2}}{2}$$

Closed formulas always make it easier to evaluate derivatives. For Asian options with arithmetical averaging, there is no exact available analytical formula. It is still possible, however, to arrive at approximations. But the best way to price these options would be to use a more advanced model based on a Monte Carlo simulation, for instance. The daily price of the underlying stock would be simulated many times from the initial date up to the expiry date. For each simulation, we calculate the implied payoff. Then the average of payoffs computed using all the simulations would lead to an expected payoff (provided the number of simulations is significant enough). Eventually, the expected payoff would be discounted to get the price of the Asian option. This process takes more time as it needs a significant number of calculations, but it is a necessary and efficient method when it comes to pricing more exotic derivatives, for which there is no available analytical pricing formula.

5 Risk Management Tools

5.1 All About the Greeks

A portfolio or fund manager needs risk management tools to be able to quantify the risks inherent in the portfolio. Indeed, if the portfolio is composed of equity derivatives, then its value depends on the variations of the different parameters that could impact the market price of these derivatives. In the case of equity options, the premium is affected by several parameters such as the actual price of the equity underlying, the volatility, the expected dividends, the interest rates and the time to maturity. There exists a series of tools or measures that help the fund manager quantify the sensitivity of the different derivatives depending on the behavior of the above parameters; these are known as the "Greeks."

In financial institutions, risk management departments often use these measures to compute the exposures of derivatives portfolios to the different market parameters. Worst case scenarios and stress tests are usually performed to estimate different risk exposures depending on different market scenarios. Limits on the different Greeks are not only given to the individual fund managers but also put in place at the global portfolio level to estimate the risks encountered by the whole organization.

Delta and Gamma

Delta

As explained previously, a derivative financial instrument is identified thus since its payoff is derived from the behavior of the underlying's price. Therefore, the derivative's price itself depends on the price of the underlying security from the inception date until the expiry date. The delta of an equity derivative instrument is its sensitivity to the variations of the underlying stock's price. The delta is the most famous Greek measure in finance. Viewed differently, a delta could be explained as follows. If the price of Stock X moves by +1$, then the value of an option written of Stock X varies by +Delta$. Mathematically, the delta of an equity derivative is equal to the first derivative of its price function with respect to the price of the underlying asset.

Using this delta definition, we can easily obtain that the delta for a stock is equal to 1. Also if we look at forward contracts, we remember from what we have seen in Chapter 3, that the value of a forward contract from the long counterparty standpoint is equal to:

$$Forward_{long}(t) = S_t \times e^{-q \times (T-t)} - K \times e^{-r \times (T-t)}$$

This theoretical price is plotted at a time t in Figure 5.1 with respect to the underlying stock's price. The strike is fixed at 100%. The time to maturity is equal to one year.

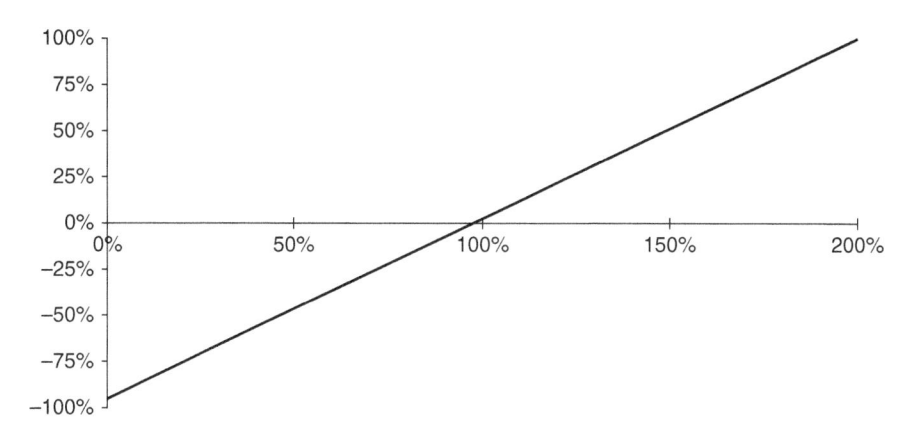

Figure 5.1 Price of a forward contract with respect to the underlying stock's price

r and q respectively represent the risk-free rate and the dividend yield, and are equal to 5% and 2%. We can see from the graph that the price of the forward contract is a linear function of the underlying stock's price (everything else constant). This implies the delta (the derivative with respect to S_t here) is constant at t and equal to

$$\Delta_{\text{Long forward}}(t) = e^{-q \times (T-t)}$$

In our example, the delta is equal to $e^{-2 \times 1\%} = 98.02\%$, almost equal to 1. In the case of stocks with no dividends, the delta of the forward contract is equal to 1. Now we can see why forward contracts, futures or swaps are often referred to as delta-one products; their deltas are almost equal to 1. Their price varies proportionally to the price of their underlying stock.

Now let's examine the delta of European calls and puts. If we derive the Black–Scholes formulas presented in Chapter 4, we get the values of the sensitivities of the prices of European call and European put with respect to the prices of the underlying stock.

$$\Delta_{\text{EuropeanCall}}(t) = e^{-q \times (T-t)} \times N(d_1)$$

and

$$\Delta_{\text{EuropeanPut}}(t) = e^{-q \times (T-t)} \times (N(d_1) - 1)$$

with

$$d_1 = \frac{\ln\left(\frac{S_T}{K}\right) + \left(r - q + \frac{\sigma^2}{2}\right) \times (T-t)}{\sigma \sqrt{T-t}}$$

$$d_2 = d_1 - \sigma \sqrt{T-t}$$

$N(x)$ is the cumulative probability up to the standardized normal value x. (More information on this function can be found in Chapter 4.) Note that $N(d_2)$ corresponds to the probability that $S_T > K$, that is, the probability that a European call expires in-the-money and equivalently that a European put expires unexercised. From the formulas above, we can observe that the deltas of European call and put options themselves depend on the following parameters: t, T, r, q, σ, K, and S_t.

Therefore, the delta is clearly not constant over time and changes from one time to another. This is an important point, as it explains why we often use the term "dynamic hedging" instead of "static hedging" in managing the risks of a portfolio.

Figure 5.2 shows the graphs of the delta value of a European call with respect to the underlying stock's price, for three different maturity dates. The strike of the call option is equal to 100% here. We can see that the values of a European call's delta always fluctuate between 0 and 1.

The delta increases as the underlying's price increases. When the call is deep out-of-the-money (when stock prices are much lower than the strike price), the delta is close to 0. This means that when the option is deep OTM there is almost no variation in the call's price, whatever the movement in the underlying stock's price; the probability of the option being exercised is so small that the value of the call becomes almost independent of the underlying's price. Conversely, when the option is deep in-the-money, the delta approaches 1. The probability of the option being exercised becomes so high that the value of the European call increases by 1\$ for every 1\$ increase in the stock's price. Then the behavior of the European call option becomes similar to that of a delta-one product.

Figure 5.2 exhibits three curves that are associated with three European call options with the same features but different maturities. Let $\Delta_{Call}(T_1)$ and $\Delta_{Call}(T_2)$ be the respective delta values at t of a European call with maturity T_1 and another European call with a higher maturity, T_2. Both call options have the same strike and are written on the same underlying price. Everything else being equal, we can see from Figure 5.2 that:

- $\Delta_{Call}(T_1) < \Delta_{Call}(T_2)$ if $S_t < K$ (Call OTM)
- $\Delta_{Call}(T_1) > \Delta_{Call}(T_2)$ if $S_t > K$ (Call ITM)

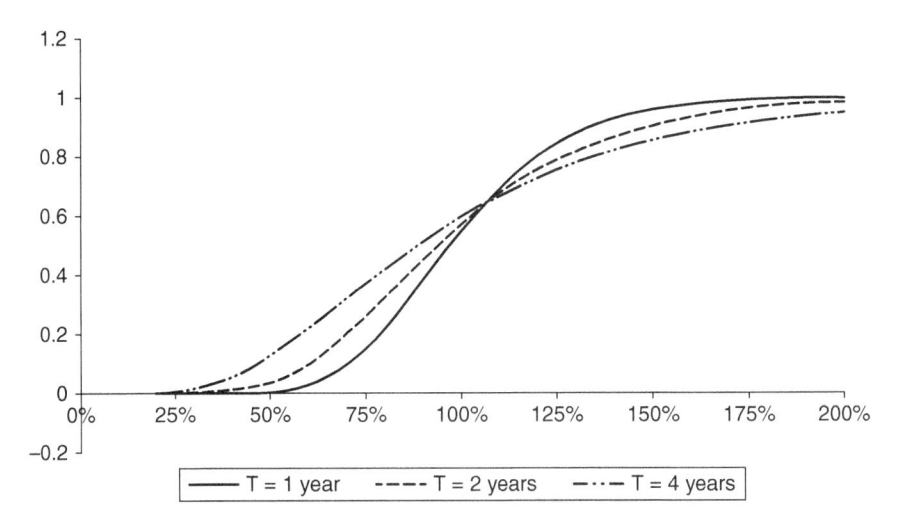

Figure 5.2 Impact of time on the delta of a European call

We can retrieve this result intuitively. If the call option is OTM, the probability of it being exercised decreases as time to maturity decreases. Then the call's value moves towards 0 (value of an unexercised call at maturity), and small moves in the underlying stock's price will have a much smaller impact on the moneyness of the option compared to a call with a much longer maturity. The latter is more sensitive to variations in the stock's price, as it has more time to change and become, for example, in-the-money.

Now if the European call option is in-the-money, time has the opposite effect; it increases the probability of the option expiring unexercised. On approaching the maturity date, the option becomes much more sensitive to the fluctuations of the stock price, as there is greater uncertainty as to whether the option will be exercised or not, that is, whether the call's price at maturity will be positive or null. That is why $\Delta_{Call}(T_1) > \Delta_{Call}(T_2)$ for in-the-money European calls, all other parameters being the same.

Figure 5.3 also compares the fluctuations of a call's delta with respect to the underlying stock's price, for different volatilities. Let $\Delta_{Call}(\sigma_1)$ and $\Delta_{Call}(\sigma_2)$ be the respective delta values at t of a European call with volatility σ_1 and another European call with a higher volatility, σ_2. Both call options have the same strike and are written on the same underlying price. Everything else being equal, we can see from Figure 5.3 that:

- $\Delta_{Call}(\sigma_1) < \Delta_{Call}(\sigma_2)$ if $S_t < K$ (Call OTM)
- $\Delta_{Call}(\sigma_1) > \Delta_{Call}(\sigma_2)$ if $S_t > K$ (Call ITM)

For equity derivatives, volatility has the same effect as time; higher volatility implies a higher probability that things will evolve in the future. From a quantitative standpoint, it is very interesting to note – and remember – that the volatility has the same impact on option prices as the square root of the time to maturity.

From Figures 5.2 and 5.3, we can also observe that the delta curve is very steep when the call is at-the-money. It can move quickly towards 0 or 1 depending on the direction

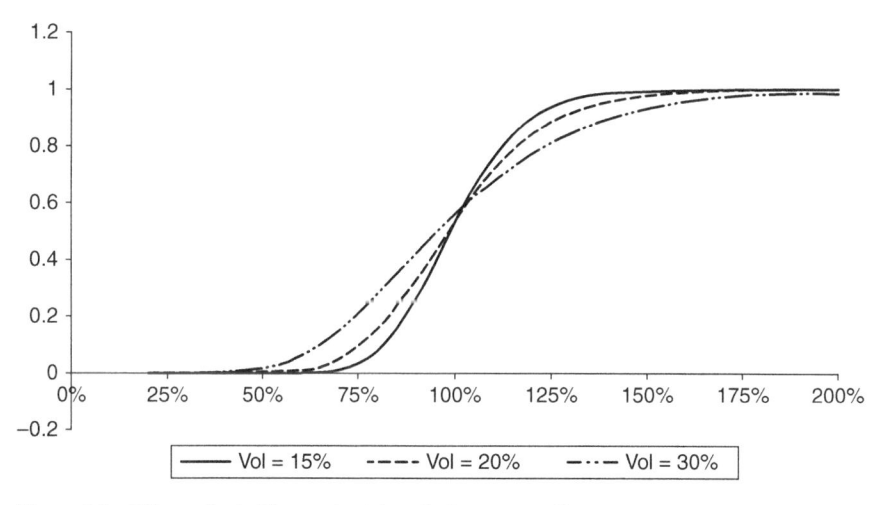

Figure 5.3 Effects of volatility on the delta of a European call

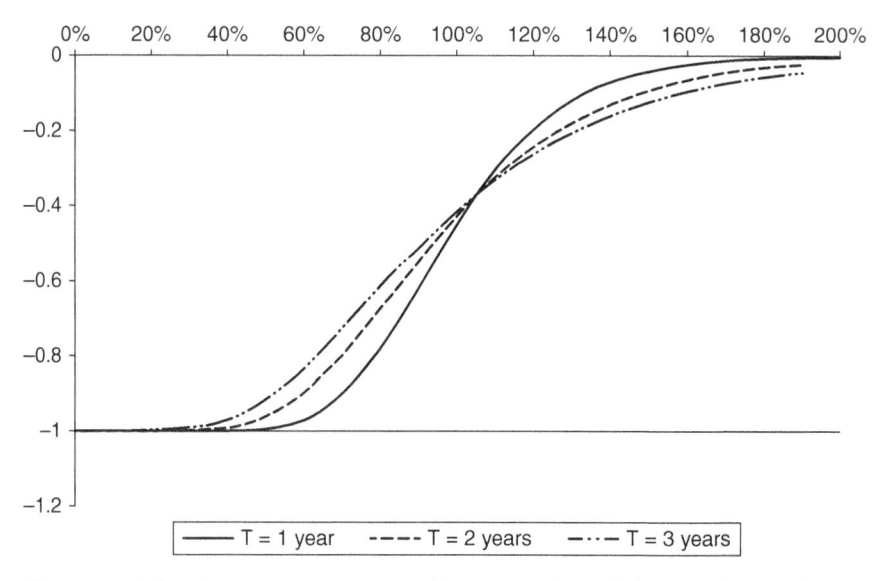

Figure 5.4 Delta of a European put option with respect to the underlying stock's price for different maturities

of the underlying stock's price. This means its derivative is maximal when underlying's price is at the strike level. We will examine this point in more detail when we discuss the Gamma, below.

Figure 5.4 shows the delta of a European put for different maturities: one, two and three years. The three options are written on the same underlying stock and have the same strike, equal to 100% of the initial spot price. Here, we have assumed a volatility of 20%, a 3% risk-free rate and a 1% dividend yield.

We can see that the values corresponding to the delta of a European put option always fluctuate between -1 and 0. The put's delta is negative and increases as the underlying's price increases. If the stock's price increases, the expected payoff of the put decreases, and the premium decreases as well. Therefore, the sensitivity of a European put option to the underlying stock's price (that is, its delta) is negative. When the call is deep out-of-the-money (stock prices are much higher than the strike price), the delta is close to 0. This means there is almost no variation in the call's price whatever the movement in the underlying stock's price; i.e. the probability of the option being exercised is so small that the value of the call becomes almost independent of the underlying's price.

Conversely, when the option is deep in-the-money, the delta approaches -1. The probability of the option being exercised becomes so high that the value of the European call increases by $1 for every $1 decrease in the stock's price. Then the behavior of the European call option becomes similar to that of, for example, a short position in a forward contract.

Figure 5.4 also exhibits three curves that are associated with three European put options with the same features but different maturities. Let $\Delta_{Put}(T_1)$ and $\Delta_{Put}(T_2)$ be the respective delta values at t of a European put with maturity T_1 and another European put with a higher maturity T_2. Both call options have the same strike and are written on the same underlying price. Everything else being equal, we can see from Figure 5.4 that:

- $\Delta_{Put}(T_1) > \Delta_{Put}(T_2)$ if $S_t < K$ (Put ITM)
- $\Delta_{Put}(T_1) < \Delta_{Put}(T_2)$ if $S_t > K$ (Put OTM)

To explain this result, we can use the same logic presented above in the case of call options.

Now let's consider a fund manager that holds 230,000 European calls on Alstom. The calls are ATM and their individual delta is almost equal to 0.5. The share price of Alstom is equal to €25. The delta for this position is computed this way: $230{,}000 \times 0.5 = 115{,}000$. This means that for every €1 negative/positive move in Alstom's share price, the value of this position decreases/increases by €115,000. If the price of Alstom shares becomes equal to €23, then the change in price is equal to −€2. Then the change in value of the long position in call options in Alstom is equal to $-€2 \times 230{,}000 \times 0.5 = -€230{,}000$. The delta gives a good risk management tool providing the exposure on the market price; it gives an idea of the potential loss in the face of adverse changes in the underlying stock's market price.

Delta Hedging

In this book, we previously explored the fact that a trader in a bank offering a European call option for their clients will in most cases hedge their position. Basically, hedging means that the aggregated value of the equity derivative position inclusive of the hedge position is constant over time, that is, no more risk is taken on, as the value of the aggregate position becomes independent of all the market parameters. Delta hedging means having a position that becomes insensitive to the underlying's market price fluctuations. In other words, the delta of the global position becomes null.

Let's continue with the example of the trader offering n European call options on Stock X. Once that trader sells call options, they compute the delta of each option Δ_{Call}; the delta of their short position in call options is then $\Delta_{Short\ Calls} = -n \times \Delta_{Call}$. The negative sign corresponds to the short position in call options. Our trader wants to delta-hedge their position totally, that is, the delta of the whole position $\Delta_{Aggregate}$ must be equal to 0. Therefore, at the same time they sell the n options, they buy a quantity of Stock X equal to Quantity $= n \times \Delta_{Call}$. The delta of the underlying stock being by construction equal to 1, then the delta of the long position in Stock X is equal to $\Delta_{long\ shares} =$ Quantity $\times 1 = n \times \Delta_{Call}$. Then the total delta of the aggregate position becomes $\Delta_{Aggregate} = \Delta_{Short\ Calls} + \Delta_{long\ shares} = 0$.

When only one hedging position is needed at the inception of trade, the hedge is said to be *static*. When we look at the evaluation formula of the delta for a European call, it appears that the delta itself depends on the underlying's price and other market parameters that vary as time goes by. If for example the stock's price goes up the next day, the delta of the short calls position will decrease (or as the delta of the individual calls increases, then $\Delta_{Aggregate}$ becomes negative). The trader will then buy a specific quantity of shares so that $\Delta_{Aggregate}$ becomes null again, and so on. Here we see that the hedge needs to be performed on a continuous basis to keep a zero-delta exposure – this is known as a *dynamic hedge*.

Earlier in this section, we saw that we can use closed-form formulas to compute the deltas for European call and put options. This is very convenient, as these are easily compiled in a program and the process is not time-consuming from a pricing perspective. Now, how would we compute a delta for a less vanilla equity derivative product? If we do not have pricing formulas for a delta of any derivative, and we obviously assume a pricing model has been developed to compute the price $P(S_t)$ of this derivative, an approximation of the delta could always be performed at time t. Mathematically, for a defined small move x in the price of the underlying stock S_t, the first derivative could be approximated by $\Delta \approx \frac{[P(S_t+x)-P(S_t)]}{x}$.

Gamma

Now that we understand that the delta is dependent on the underlying stock's price, we can deduct that the trader willing to delta-hedge his portfolio has to dynamically adjust his hedge depending on the change in the delta. It is then important to quantify how sensitive the delta is to the price of the underlying equity asset. The gamma measures the sensitivity of the delta with respect to the underlying stock's price; a high gamma indicates that the trader needs to adjust his hedge on a frequent basis.

Mathematically, the gamma is the first derivative of the delta with respect to the price of the underlying asset. It is also equal to the second derivative of a financial product's price function with respect to the price of the underlying asset. The gamma measures the convexity of the price curve with respect to the price of the underlying equity asset. For delta-one products such as stocks, ETFs, futures, forwards and swaps, the delta does not depend on S_t at any point of time t. Therefore, the gamma of delta-one products is equal to 0. This also means that the delta-hedge for these financial products is static only.

If the underlying stock varies significantly, then the delta in the case of options will change frequently, implying a high gamma. Intuitively, the gamma would be high for options on volatile stocks, and low for options written on stable equity assets. As is the case for the delta, we can found closed-form formulas to evaluate the gamma of European options:

$$\Gamma_{EuropeanOption}(t) = \frac{e^{-q \times (T-t)} \times N'(d_1)}{S_t \times \sigma \sqrt{T-t}}$$

where

$$N'(x) = \frac{e^{\frac{-x^2}{2}}}{\sqrt{2\Pi}}$$

The gamma of a European call option is equal to the gamma of a European put. To prove this result, we come back to the put/call parity formula:

$$\text{Call}(t) - \text{Put}(t) = \text{Forward}_{Long}(t)$$

By deriving this equation twice with respect to S_t, we obtain:

$$\Gamma_{EuropeanCall}(t) - \Gamma_{EuropeanPut}(t) = \Gamma_{Forward}(t)$$

And since $\Gamma_{Forward} = 0$,

$$\Gamma_{EuropeanCall}(t) = \Gamma_{EuropeanPut}(t)$$

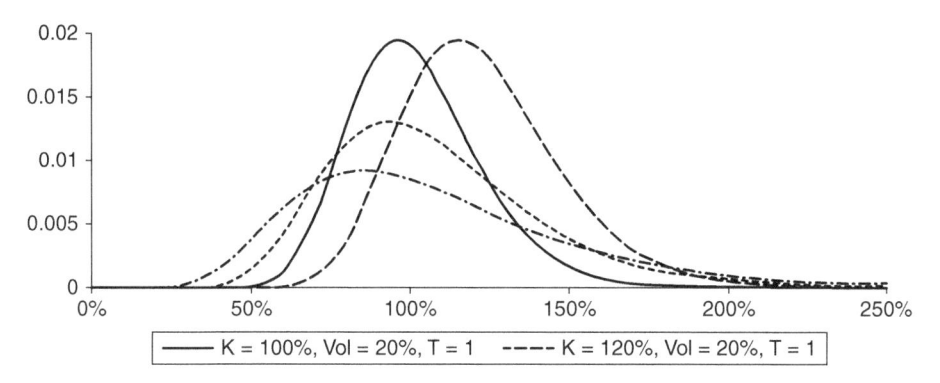

Figure 5.5 Gamma of a European option with respect to the underlying stock's price for different maturities

Note that if we differentiate once the call/put parity, we get

$$\Delta_{Call} = \Delta_{Put} + e^{-q \times (T-t)}$$

The gamma of a European call or put is always positive. We can see this from the graph representing the price of European options with respect to the underlying asset, as the curve is convex – so the second derivative is positive. For vanilla options, it usually fluctuates between 0 and 0.1. Long positions in European calls have a positive gamma, and short positions in European options are said to be negative gamma. A gamma of 0.05 signifies that the delta increases by 0.05 for a European call or a European put, when the market price of the underlying equity appreciates by 1.

Figure 5.5 shows the evolution of the gamma for a European call option with strike at 110% and different maturities. We can see that the gamma reaches a maximum when the spot price is equal to the strike price. Remember the delta curve is steepest at the strike level. The gamma is almost null when the option is OTM or ITM. This means the delta is almost constant (−1 or 0 for a put; 0 or 1 for a call). Figure 5.5 also compares the gammas depending on the time to expiry. For shorter maturities, the evolution of gamma is more aggressive. As time approaches the expiry date, the gamma becomes more sensitive to the time and the trader needs to adjust his exposure and hedge more frequently. When options are at-the-money, the ones with a shorter time to maturity have a higher gamma. The opposite situation happens when options are ITM or OTM.

Eventually, we can approximate the gamma for any kind of equity derivative using the following method. For a predetermined small move x in the price of the underlying stock S_t, the gamma could be computed as $\Gamma \approx \dfrac{[\Delta(S_t+x) - \Delta(S_t)]}{x}$.

Vega and Theta

Vega

The vega calculates the sensitivity of an equity derivative price to the volatility of its underlying. From a mathematical standpoint, it represents the first derivative of the price of a specific derivative instrument with respect to the volatility. As studied previously, the price of futures or forwards does not depend on the underlying asset's volatility; therefore, the vega of delta-one products in general is equal to 0. For options though, the vega is a crucial measure, as volatility is probably the most important parameter to manage when trading these products.

For European calls and puts, the higher the volatility the higher the premium. Indeed, the expected payoff increases with volatility, as the payoff of a European option is asymmetric. The investor buying European options is said to be long volatility of the underlying stock. If volatility increases, then the value of their options holdings would increase. Conversely, the seller of options is short volatility. The vega measures the exposure of a portfolio of options to the volatility factor. If a particular underlying stock has a volatility of 18%, a vega of 0.25 means that the premium in the money amount increases by $0.25 \times 2\% = 0.005$ if the volatility becomes equal to 20%.

In the case of equity European options, the call and put with the same features have the same vega:

$$\text{Vega}_{\text{EuropeanOption}}(t) = S_t \times e^{-q \times (T-t)} \times N'(d_1) \times \sqrt{T-t}$$

where

$$N'(x) = \frac{e^{-\frac{x^2}{2}}}{\sqrt{2\Pi}}$$

As is the case for the gamma, the vega of a European call option is equal to the vega of a European put. To prove this result, we once again base our logic on deriving the put/call parity with respect to the volatility now:

$$\text{Call}(t) - \text{Put}(t) = \text{Forward}_{\text{long}}(t)$$

By deriving this equation twice with respect to σ, we obtain:

$$\text{Vega}_{\text{EuropeanCall}}(t) - \text{Vega}_{\text{EuropeanPut}}(t) = \text{Vega}_{\text{Forward}}(t)$$

And since $\text{Vega}_{\text{Forward}} = 0$,

$$\text{Vega}_{\text{EuropeanCall}}(t) = \text{Vega}_{\text{EuropeanPut}}(t)$$

From the Black–Scholes formula of the vega above, we can observe that the vega is not constant, varying with time and the underlying's price itself. Also $N'(d_1)$ is always positive; this implies that the vega is always positive. This result is consistent with the fact that the price of a European option increases as volatility increases.

In Figure 5.6, the vega of a European put option is plotted against the underlying equity price. Also, three curves are drawn to show the effect of time on the vega of three different puts written on the same stock, with the same strike (at 100% of the initial spot price) but different maturity dates. For a given expiry date, the vega is greatest when the option is at-the-money, and decays exponentially on both sides as the option becomes OTM or ITM, thus giving the bell-shaped curve in Figure 5.6. When the spot price is at the level of the strike, a higher volatility could make the option give a much higher payoff with time (if it ends in-the-money), or 0 (if it ends out-of-the-money). This is why the vega for higher maturity options is higher.

It is very important for an equity trader to take into account the variation of the value of their portfolio in function of the volatility of the different underlying

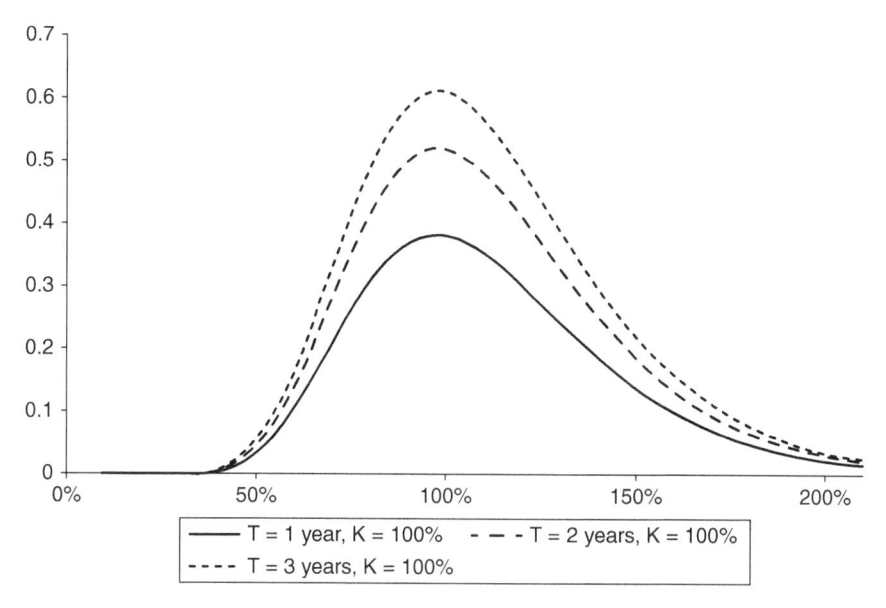

Figure 5.6 Vega of a European put option with respect to the underlying stock's price for different maturities

securities. In the case of a portfolio composed of long positions in options written on the CAC 40 index, for instance, the volatility risk is the risk that the portfolio value will decrease if the volatility of CAC 40 decreases. Let's assume the actual volatility of the CAC 40 index is 20%, and that an index point is equivalent to €10. Also, let's assume the level of the CAC 40 is at 3600 points. Then take an average vega of 5 for a portfolio of long positions in 250 options. The vega of the portfolio could be computed as 250 × 5 = 1250. Expressed in cash terms, it is equal to 1,250 × €10 = €12,500. This means that everything else being equal, if the volatility of CAC 40 decreases to 19%, the portfolio's value decreases by €12,500.

Risk departments will apply vega limits on options portfolios to ensure that this volatility risk will remain under control. A high vega implies a high exposure to changes in volatility. Remember that a long position in European options has a positive vega and a short position a negative vega. Therefore, the vega of a portfolio could be increased or decreased, and thus controlled, by buying or selling options.

Theta

The theta is the speed at which an equity derivative varies over time, all other parameters being constant. It is the first derivative of the price function of a specific derivative instrument with respect to time. For European options, the higher the time to maturity the higher the expected payoff, and thus the higher the premium. Similarly, the premium for options decreases as time goes by. This is why options are usually called wasting assets. They have a limited life and if all market parameters remain constant, their value is meant to decrease with time. Note, however, that this is not always the case, as there are very specific situations where the theta of an option could be positive; this special case will be explored later in this section.

The theta is then most often negative for long positions in European options and positive for short positions. The theta gives the decrease in an option's value for a period of one year if all the other parameters such as volatility, the underlying's price, the risk-free rate and the dividend yield do not change. So to measure the one-day theta, divide the computed theta by 365; for a week, multiply theta by 7/365, and so on. The buyer of an option is short theta, meaning they prefer the theta to be small in order not to lose too much value due to the erosion of time. Alternatively, the option seller is long theta and wants the value of the sold option to decrease and end up unexercised to gain the premium.

Under Black–Scholes assumptions, the theta for a European call and put with strike K and maturity T are:

$$\Theta_{EuropeanCall}(t) = \frac{-S_t \times \sigma \times e^{-q \times (T-t)} \times N'(d_1)}{2\sqrt{T-t}} - r \times K \times e^{-q \times (T-t)} \times N(d_2)$$
$$+ q \times S_t \times e^{-q \times (T-t)} \times N(d_1)$$

and

$$\Theta_{EuropeanPut}(t) = \frac{-S_t \times \sigma \times e^{-q \times (T-t)} \times N'(d_1)}{2\sqrt{T-t}} + r \times K \times e^{-q \times (T-t)} \times N(-d_2)$$
$$- q \times S_t \times e^{-q \times (T-t)} \times N(-d_1)$$

where

$$N'(x) = \frac{e^{\frac{-x^2}{2}}}{\sqrt{2\Pi}}$$

Looking at the equations above and using the property that $N(x) = 1 - N(-x)$, we can rewrite

$$\Theta_{EuropeanPut}(t) = \Theta_{EuropeanCall}(t) + r \times K \times e^{-r \times (T-t)} - q \times S_t \times e^{-q \times (T-t)}$$

This relationship could also be verified using the put/call parity. Figure 5.7 shows the curve of the theta for a European call plotted against the underlying stock's price for different maturities. The strike is at 90%, and σ, r and q are set at 30%, 5% and 0% respectively. The first thing to note is that the theta for a call is always non-positive. The maximum absolute value for the theta occurs the option is at-the-money. As the premium of an OTM call is quite cheap, the effect of time becomes not so important and thus the theta is quite low. For longer maturities, call options have a lower absolute theta when the spot is around the strike price, and a higher absolute theta otherwise.

Now let's study how the theta varies in the case of European put. Figure 5.8 shows the effects of time and spot price on the theta of a European put. The strike is at 110%, and σ, r and q are set at 30%, 5% and 2% respectively. Here, we can observe that the absolute value of the theta reaches its maximum when the call is at-the-money and time to maturity is low. Like call options, puts with longer maturities have a lower absolute theta when the spot is around the strike price, and a higher absolute theta otherwise.

It is important to note that the theta for a European put could be positive when the spot price is much lower than the strike, that is, when the put is deep in-the-money.

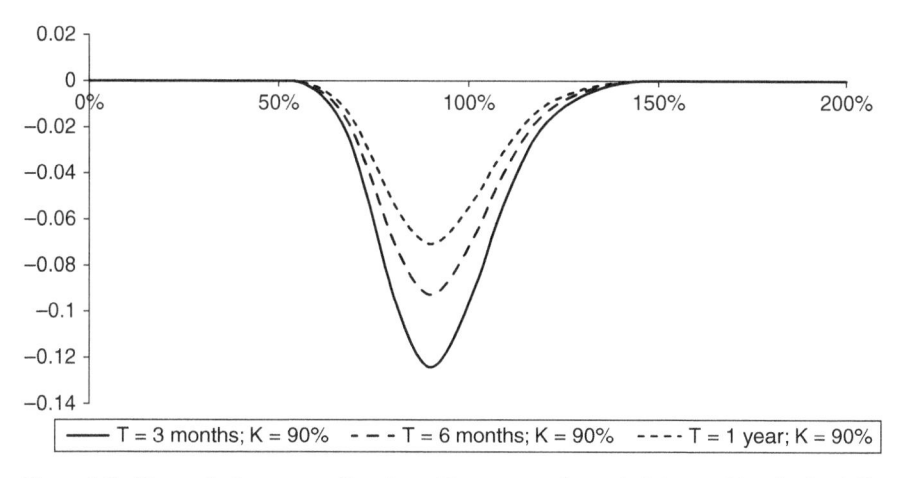

Figure 5.7 Theta of a European call option with respect to the underlying stock's price for different maturities

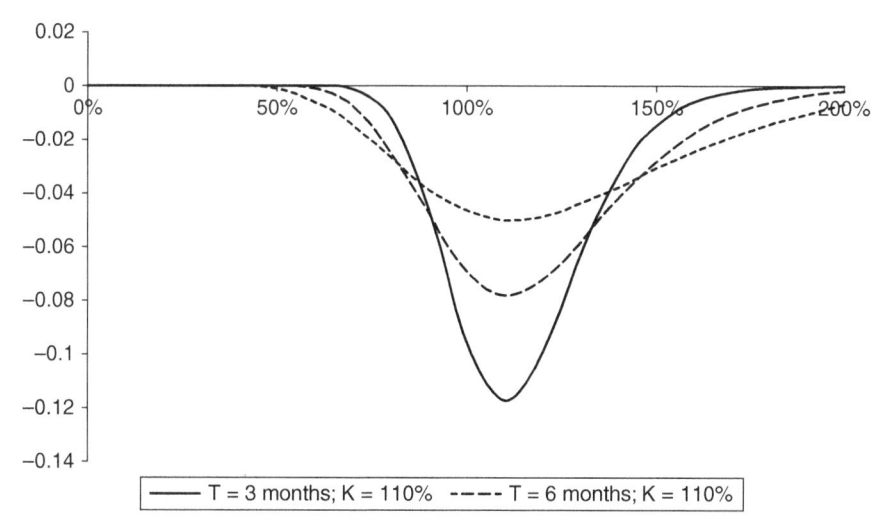

Figure 5.8 Theta of a European put option with respect to the underlying stock's price for different maturities

This special situation happens due to the effect of discounting on the strike that decreases the premium. So when time decreases, the discounted strike is higher and the premium higher, resulting in a positive theta. This result could be understood in a very intuitive way too. Remember that in the case of European put options, the maximum payoff is finite and equal to the strike price; this happens when the spot is almost equal to 0. So when a put option is deep-in-the-money, the payoff cannot increase much more, and the maximum payoff is almost reached. If the time approaches maturity, the value of the option gets higher, as there is a greater probability of receiving this high payoff.

Traders and portfolio managers must control the effect of time on their portfolio. Say a trader buys 200 calls on CAC 40 index with the strike at 3600 points and a daily theta (computed as theta/365) of −0.92, plus 300 calls on the same index but with a strike at 3650 and a daily theta of −0.87; the global theta of their position is equal to $200 \times (-0.92) + 300 \times (-0.87) = -445$. Assuming 1 point of this French index is equivalent to €10, the daily theta in euro terms is equal to $-445 \times €10 = -€4450$. This means the value of this position will decrease by €4450 the next day if all other parameters remain constant. As is usually with the other Greeks, limits are also applied to portfolios in terms of theta. It is interesting to note that the time is the only parameter that is not market-dependent. Its evolution cannot be controlled, but its exposure could be limited.

Rho

The rho is the sensitivity of an equity derivative's price with respect to the risk-free rate. The rho measures by how much the price of the equity derivative changes for a 1% increase in interest rates. For instance, if we derive a forward contract value by the interest rate, we obtain:

$$\text{Rho}_{\text{LongForward}}(t) = K \times (T-t) \times e^{-r \times (T-t)}$$

The rho is positive for a long forward position, i.e. the value of the forward contract increases if interest rates increase. For the short position in a forward contract, the rho is the negative of the formula above.

For options now, the risk-free rate is not a very important parameter to be risk managed. Its impact on the option's value is quite low. However, it could be measured by the rho. Under Black–Scholes assumptions, the rho for a European call and put with strike K and maturity T are:

$$\text{Rho}_{\text{EuropeanCall}}(t) = K \times (T-t) \times e^{-r \times (T-t)} \times N(d_2)$$

and

$$\text{Rho}_{\text{EuropeanPut}}(t) = K \times (T-t) \times e^{-r \times (T-t)} \times [N(d_2) - 1]$$

Looking at these formulas, we can clearly observe that the rho for a European call option is always positive. In Figure 5.9, the rho of a European call is plotted against the spot price for different maturities. Note that the strike price is at 100%. If the risk-free rate increases, then the price of a call increases. Indeed a higher interest rate increases the potential forward price, which in turn increases the expected payoff. At the same time, the discount rate is higher and has the opposite effect on the call's premium. Now the positive effect on the forward is higher in absolute terms compared to the negative effect of the discounting (as the strike is also discounted). Therefore, the aggregate impact of the increase interest rates is an increase in the call's premium.

For a European put option, the rho is negative and the proof is more straightforward. In a financial environment with increasing interest rates, the expected forward price decreases, and the effect of discounting has also a negative impact on the value of the European put. Figure 5.10 shows the rho of a European put option with a strike at 100% for two different maturities. The rho is clearly negative, and time has an impact on the value of the rho. In absolute terms, the rho is greater for a European option

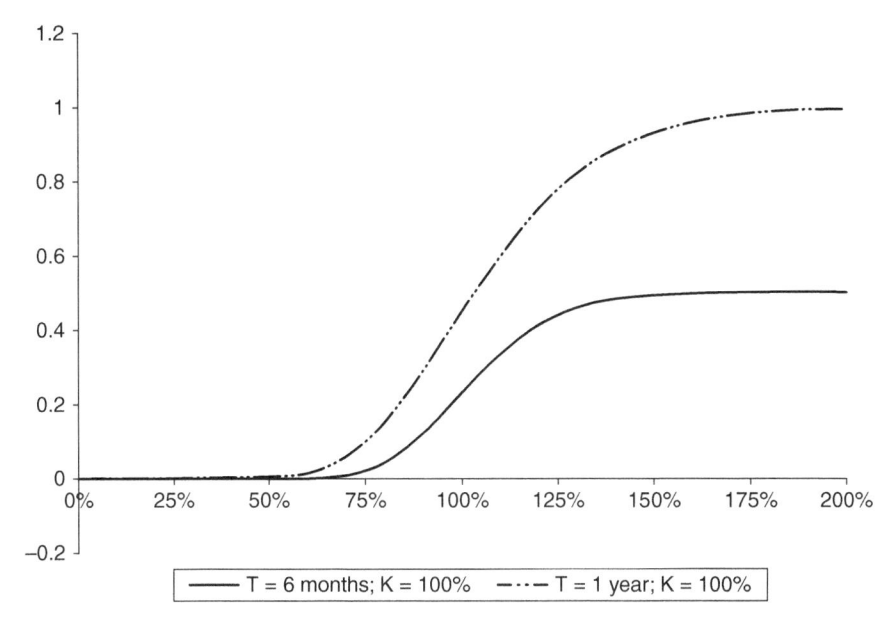

Figure 5.9 Rho of a European call option with respect to the underlying stock's price for different maturities

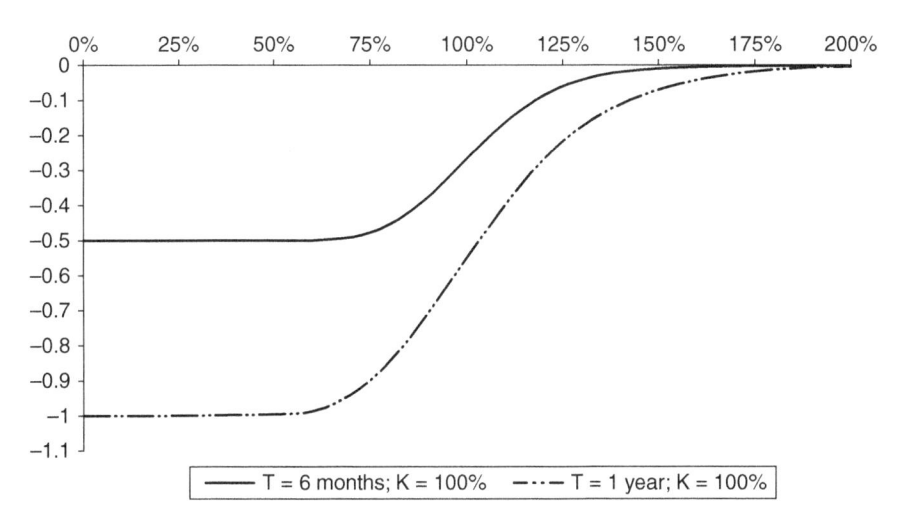

Figure 5.10 Rho of a European put option with respect to the underlying stock's price for different maturities

with a higher maturity. Also, the absolute value of the rho increases as the moneyness of the option increases. When the European option is deep OTM, the rho is almost null, and interest rates have no significant impact on the option's price.

In emerging countries where interest rates can change significantly, market makers and traders should also take into account the impact of these variations on their options portfolios. In practice, however, the rho is not really managed intensively as its value is usually quite low compared to the other Greeks. It is not often the case when the risk controllers insist on establishing strict limits for the rho exposure.

Volga and Vanna

The most important Greeks in risk management are the delta, gamma, vega, theta and rho. In this section, we present additional sensitivities, the volga and the vanna, that are much less well known but can be important in sophisticated derivatives portfolios. We will analyze the essentials briefly, giving a brief description of them.

Volga

The volga is the first derivative of the vega with respect to the volatility of the underlying asset. It is the second-order sensitivity of a financial product's price function to the volatility movements of the underlying equity asset. An option is said to exhibit vega-convexity if the volga is not equal to 0. On plotting the graphs of the prices of ATM, OTM and ITM European calls and puts against the volatility, it can be observed that these curves are not linear and are convex in volatility.

In the case of more exotic structures such as Napoleons or cliquets, the volga is so important that it needs to be controlled in order to protect the portfolio from unexpected losses. An option with a vega convex payoff will see its vega changing as the underlying's volatility changes. The models used for pricing must take these impacts into account in order to price these risks accordingly.

Vanna

The vanna measures the sensitivity of the delta to a change in volatility; or from a different perspective, it is the sensitivity of the vega to a movement in the underlying equity's price. As it is the case for the volga, the vanna is also a second-order sensitivity, as it is the derivative of the derivative's price with respect to a simultaneous change in the underlying's price and volatility.

For a trader performing a delta-hedge, the vanna provides useful information, as it tells us by how much the hedge position changes depending on movements in the volatility. Conversely, for practitioners undertaking vega hedging, the vanna provides the sensitivity of the vega to changes in the underlying's price.

If the vanna is very low, then there is no need to pay it much attention. If, however, its value becomes large, then the delta-hedge becomes highly sensitive to movements of volatility; and the vega-hedge is strongly impacted by changes in the underlying's price.

5.2 Greeks Closed Relationships

Previously in this chapter, we saw that there exist relationships between the same Greeks of a European put and call. These results are directly derived from the put/call parity. Now we are going to explore the relationships between the different Greeks of the same equity derivative. Under Black–Scholes assumptions, we get the following formulas at any time t during the life of a European option:

$$\Theta_{\text{Call}} + r \times S_t \times \Delta_{\text{Call}} + \tfrac{1}{2} \times \sigma^2 \times S_t^2 \times \Gamma_{\text{Call}} = r \times \text{Premium}_{\text{Call}}(t)$$

and

$$\Theta_{Put} + r \times S_t \times \Delta_{Put} + \frac{1}{2} \times \sigma^2 \times S_t^2 \times \Gamma_{Put} = r \times \text{Premium}_{Put}(t)$$

From these relationships, we can observe the trade-off between the sensitivities to movements in the price (delta and gamma) and the time effect (theta) on the price of a European option. Note that $\text{Premium}_{Call}(t)$ and $\text{Premium}_{Put}(t)$ represent the values of a European call and a European put at time t respectively.

Positions in Gamma, Delta and Theta for a European Call

Consider a trader in a bank offering European call options on a quantity n of Stock X to one of their clients. We previously said that these traders are not supposed to be gamblers; they do not take naked positions, speculating on the behavior of a specific stock. Therefore, they usually hedge their position totally, at least delta-wise. So, immediately after selling the call options, the trader buys a quantity $n \times \Delta_{Call}$ of Stock X; where Δ_{Call} represents the computed delta at the trade date of each individual European call. This way, the global delta of the aggregate position {Short calls and hedge} is equal to 0.

Whenever the stock goes up, the delta of the calls increases, then the global delta goes from 0 to negative. To push it back up to 0, the trader buys back a number of shares equal to this change of delta. If the share price decreases, Δ_{Call} decreases and the global delta becomes positive. To bring it back down to 0, the trader needs to sell a specific quantity of Stock X. To summarize, the dynamic delta hedging for a call option seller implies buying stocks expensive (when their price increases) and selling them cheap (when their price decreases). Therefore the hedge becomes costly when the stock's price varies significantly. This is why the trader selling a call is said to be short gamma, meaning they prefer the realized volatility to decrease. Conversely, the call option buyer is said to be long gamma, as its hedge involves buying the underlying stock cheap and selling it expensive through the life of the option. Eventually, a call option seller is short gamma, long theta, and the opposite situation happens for a call option buyer.

Positions in Gamma, Delta and Theta for a European Put

In the case of a trader selling European put options to a bank's client, assume the puts are written on n shares of Stock X. Here again we consider a trader that fully delta-hedges their position, intending to remove their exposure to the movements in the underlying stock's price. The delta for each European put option is negative and fluctuates in the range $[-1; 0]$. When the put is at-the-money, its delta is around -0.5. As the trader is the seller of options here, then they create a delta-positive position. To keep the portfolio delta-neutral, the trader needs to short-sell a quantity of Stock X equal to $-n \times \Delta_{Put}$ at the trade date.

As time goes by, an increase in the price of Stock X is accompanied by an increase in Δ_{Put}, which still remains negative but lower in absolute value. This positive change in delta implies that the global delta becomes negative. This means the put seller needs to buy back shares of Stock X to push the delta of the aggregate position back to 0. The opposite happens when the underlying stock decreases in value. All in all, for a

European put option seller, the hedge consists of buying expensive and selling cheap. Here again the investor or trader selling a European put option is said to be short the gamma and long the theta; conversely, a put option buyer is long the gamma and short the theta.

EXERCISE

Fadia Chakib is a successful trader that works for a top-tier investment bank. She manages options portfolios and most often applies a 100% delta-hedge for her positions. One of her sub-portfolios is composed of short positions in European call options written on Stock Y, denominated in USD. This sub-portfolio is fully delta-hedged today. Let's also assume this portfolio's daily theta is $\Theta_{1d} = \$3500$. Also, the implied volatility and the interest rates are constant in this example. Considering that the realized volatility of Stock Y is equal to 24%, what would the daily P&L of the sub-portfolio be if the stock moves by +3% during the next trading day?

Discussion

The daily profit and loss $P\&L_{1d}$ corresponds to the change in the value of the sub-portfolio. Let's consider the respective values V_0 and V_1 of the sub-portfolio today and the following day. Using the definitions of the different Greeks we have studied above, we obtain:

$$V_1 - V_0 = \Theta_{1d} \times \delta t + \text{Rho}_{1d} \times \delta r + \text{Vega}_{1d} \times \delta\sigma_{implied} + \Delta_{1d} \times \delta S + \tfrac{1}{2} \times \Gamma_{1d} \times \delta s^2$$

The risk-free rate and implied volatility are assumed to be constant; so the change in rates $\delta r = 0$ and the change in implied volatility $\delta\sigma_{implied} = 0$.

Moreover, the portfolio is fully delta-hedged, meaning the global delta of the portfolio Δ_{1d} is null. And $\delta t = 1$ for a one-day period.

We then get:

$$P\&L_{1d} = V_1 - V_0 = \Theta_{1d} + \tfrac{1}{2} \times \Gamma_{1d} \times \delta s^2$$

Since the portfolio is delta-neutral, the gain from the theta should be offset by the loss in gamma, assuming a realized volatility of 24%. In this case, Fadia Chakib is long theta and short gamma, i.e. she makes money when the spot of the underlying stock does not move much. The breakeven daily P&L happens when the daily realized volatility of Stock Y is equal to $\sigma_{1d} = \frac{24\%}{\sqrt{252}} = 1.5\%$. For the ease of computations, remember that $\sqrt{252}$ is almost equal to 16.

In the case of a breakeven daily P&L, we get from the above formula:

$$\Theta_{1d} + \tfrac{1}{2} \times \Gamma_{1d} \times \sigma_{1d}^2 = 0$$

and

$$\tfrac{1}{2} \times \Gamma_{1d} \times \sigma_{1d}^2 = -3500 \text{ USD}$$

Now if the stock price moves by 3%, this means $\delta S = 2 \times \sigma_{1d}$
If we replace the parameters by their actual values in the above P&L formula, we obtain:

$$P\&L_{1d} = \Theta_{1d} + \tfrac{1}{2} \times \Gamma_{1d} \times (2 \times \sigma_{1d})^2$$

Then
$$\text{P\&L}_{1d} = 3,500 + 4 \times \left\{\tfrac{1}{2} \times \Gamma_{1d} \times \sigma_{1d}^2\right\}$$

And since $\tfrac{1}{2} \times \Gamma_{1d} \times \sigma_{1d} = -3500$ USD

$$\text{P\&L}_{1d} = 3,500 + 4 \times (-3,500) = -10,500 \text{ USD}$$

So Fadia Chakib would suffer a loss of $10,500 as she is short gamma, and the price of Stock Y has varied by twice the breakeven threshold.

5.3 Choosing the Right Model

The idea behind this chapter is to present the main Greeks used as risk management tools. We have seen how useful they can be in computing the exposure of a portfolio of derivatives to the variations of the different parameters that impact its value. These sensitivities need to be evaluated and if found important they may be risk managed with careful attention. Models must be chosen for every type of derivative depending on its Greeks, in order to be able to capture all these sensitivities and incorporate them into the price of the derivative.

Always remember as a fundamental rule that the price (net of any additional fees) of any derivative should be equal to the cost of hedging it. The objective of a model is to anticipate how the value of the derivative in the portfolio is likely to vary depending on the time and the other market parameters. So the model must be able to show not only the variations of the equity underlying throughout the life of the derivative but also how the price is going to move and react to changes in these parameters.

In the case of delta-one products or European options, closed-form formulas are often used for pricing. This proves to be very convenient as there are no iterations to be done, so the pricer provides an almost instantaneous price. Note that some very exotic path-dependent options can take hours to be priced by computers, as they need hundreds of thousands of calculations. For European options, the Black–Scholes model has been used for quite some time. Many assumptions in this model are false; however, this model is still seen by many as the right one to use for these derivatives. This may be quite controversial, but finds its explanation in the heart of the definition for a model. Always keep in mind that a good model is one that provides a theoretical price that follows the market price best. The Black–Scholes model for pricing European options is so popular that most of market participants use it to post their bids and asks in the market. By construction it becomes a model that gives an output close to the market prices.

When we have to evaluate the value of more complicated options, we will need to use more advanced models such as binomial trees or Monte Carlo simulations to get a good pricing. Exotic options are often path-dependent; their payoff is dependent on the path taken by the underlying equity asset throughout from inception and until maturity date. Note that for European options, only the price at maturity is important. For non-vanilla derivatives, a model is needed that draws the evolution of all the market parameters for the whole product life, in order to have an expected value of a complicated payoff. In the case of a Monte Carlo simulation, different paths are drawn to get a single payoff sample; this process is repeated thousands of times to get a series of potential payoffs. Their average is computed to approximate the expected payoff value; then this value is discounted, to obtain the price for the product. This may be very time-consuming in practice, as it could involve a very large number of calculations.

Basically, in order to compute the price of a derivative, we can compute the expected payoff and then discount it. But what rate should be used to compute the payoff expected value and its discounted value simultaneously? The answer depends on the degree of risk aversion in the investors. In the Black–Scholes theory, it has been proven that the price of a derivative is not a function of the investor's required return for a specific underlying security. This means that the pricing of a derivative would be the same for all risk-averse environments – we just need to decide on a particular risk environment and use its associated risk-adjusted required return. In order to simplify computations only, we usually assume that we are in a risk-neutral environment, that is, investors require the risk-free rate for all securities. This has been implicitly assumed in this book, as we discount the expected values with the risk-free rate.

The model is at the heart of the pricing and must be carefully chosen for every type of derivative. If the model used to evaluate a large portfolio is incorrect, the difference between the market price and the computed theoretical price can be quite significant, and may result in substantial losses. In practice, experienced traders are knowledgeable about the different sensitivities of the options they trade and will use the right models to capture all the effects of the different parameters in order to obtain a proper valuation. In the case of new structured products, structurers work closely with the quantitative analysts and the traders to validate the right model. Then tests are carried out to stress the different market parameters and correctly identify the behavior of the new financial product.

6 Strategies Built around Vanillas

6.1 Equity Hedging the Traditional Way

Covered Calls

A short covered call strategy is particularly appreciated by portfolio managers. Indeed, they can choose to adopt short-, medium- or long-term strategies. In the case of funds following longer-term strategies, they may need to keep their holdings when stock markets are going down. This does not happen without impacting the portfolio's valuation; investors may feel uneasy in these situations, and thus may withdraw their money from the fund even if portfolio managers try to explain that it is part of their strategy, as they believe the market will bounce back. Therefore, portfolio and fund managers usually sell equity call options during periods when they believe the underlying stock will decrease. As the options' time to maturity corresponds to the length of these periods, the premium they get for selling the call options would compensate for the unrealized loss from holding the underperforming stocks during that time.

Adopting this strategy is known as "following a short covered call strategy"; that is, holding a portfolio composed of a short position in a call option and a long position in the underlying stock. The payoff at maturity from a short covered call position for one stock is equal to:

$$Payoff_{ShortCoveredCall} = -Max\{0, S_T - K\} + S_T$$

and the profit from this strategy is equal to:

$$\operatorname{Pr}ofit_{ShortCoveredCall} = Premium_{Call} - Max\{0, S_T - K\} + S_T - S_0$$

or

$$\operatorname{Pr}ofit_{ShortCoveredCall} = \begin{cases} Premium_{Call} + K - S_0 \\ Premium_{Call} + S_T - S_0 \end{cases} \text{if} \quad \begin{matrix} S_T > K \\ S_T \leq K \end{matrix}$$

Basically, this strategy is followed for two main reasons – (a) to offset the loss from a small short-term decrease in the stock price or (b) to increase a portfolio's rate of return in the case of an anticipated stability of prices in the short-term.

(a) Partially offsetting the loss from an expected short-term slight decrease in the underlying stock's price:

The strike of the sold call is determined according to the manager's expectations. In this scenario, the trader believes the stock's price will slightly decrease and will not increase up to a particular threshold; then the implied strike would usually be

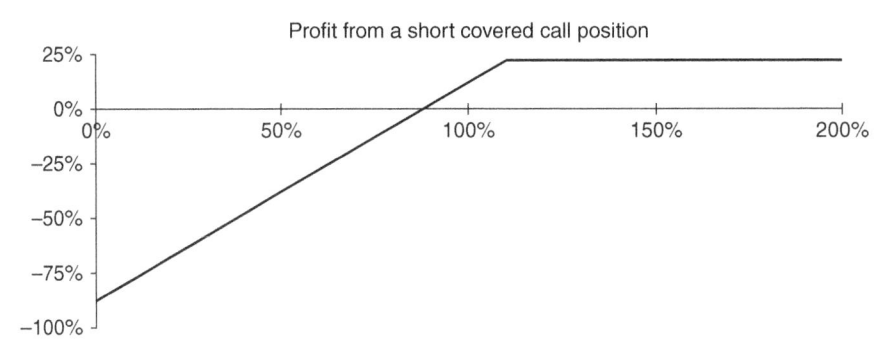

Figure 6.1 Profit graph from a short covered call position

higher than this threshold. Most often, calls are offered out-of-the-money as shown in Figure 6.1. The strike is at 110% of the initial spot price and the three-month call's premium is equal to 12%. The lower the strike, the higher the premium, but the risk of the call option being exercised is higher. So there is always this risk/return balance that needs to be adjusted according to market expectations and the risk appetite of the fund manager.

There are two possible scenarios when following this strategy. First, if the price of a particular stock in the portfolio decreases as predicted during the life of the call, the sold call written on this share is not exercised, and the gain for the portfolio manager is equal to the premium, which partially compensates for the loss from the underlying share. In the strategy exhibited in Figure 6.1, the loss is totally offset up to a 12% decrease in the underlying stock's price. Otherwise, any loss is partially decreased by the premium of 12%. For example, if the stock's price has decreased by 18% after three months, the total P&L of the portfolio is equal to $-18\% + 12\% = -6\%$.

Now let's consider the other scenario where the expectations of the portfolio manager are proved to be wrong and the stock's price increases instead of decreasing. Then the call's value increases as the stock's price increases, and the gain from the underlying share's positive performance will be offset by the loss incurred from the short call position. Thus the portfolio's value will not profit from an increasing market above the strike price; in the case shown in Figure 6.1, the maximum profit is locked to $Premium + K - S_0$; i.e. $12\% + 110\% - 100\% = 22\%$. In practice, when a fund manager observes an increasing market they do not wait until the expiry date to take action; before the stock price reaches the strike price, the manager usually buys back the call option they offered, and sells another one with a higher strike (at a lower price) to make sure they will not have to deliver their shares. This is called "rolling a position." This operation is repeated as often as needed, and obviously incurs losses for the fund manager.

(b) *Increasing the portfolio's total return in the case of an anticipated stability in the underlying stock's price:*

The portfolio manager sells OTM call options when he believes the stock's price will be stable or slightly increase. As explained previously, he rolls the position by buying their original sold call and selling new calls with a higher strike whenever the underlying's price approaches the strike. When the underlying stock is significantly volatile, positions would have to be rolled many times, which can be very costly; this is one of the reasons why the short covered calls strategy is normally only used for shares with low volatility. Obviously, the premium received would be low as well.

Eventually, if the underlying share's price is expected to decrease slightly in the short-term, the sold calls could be at-the-money or even in-the-money (higher premium). The maximum potential loss is decreased by the premium of the sold call. This strategy enables the fund manager to partially hedge the portfolio from a possibly underperforming stock market during a particular period. Figure 6.1 shows that the maximum loss from this strategy may be very substantial in the case of a significant downside in the underlying stock's price; it would have been better to have sold the stocks even with high trading costs. That is why the short covered calls strategy is not a true hedging strategy, as it proves to be very inefficient in the case of significant market moves. It is important to note that this strategy works better in a stable market.

Protective Puts

A long protective put strategy consists of holding a share plus a European put written on the underlying stock. The idea is to protect the equity portfolio from downside market movements during specific periods. Most often, a portfolio manager would adopt a protective put strategy as a hedging tool to lock the potential loss to a particular level.

Let T be the maturity date of the bought put option; T corresponds to the end date of the period during which the manager wishes to gain protection against a decrease in the underlying stock's price. The put's strike, K, is determined according to the portfolio's risk constraints. Indeed the equity portfolio is totally hedged below the strike level. The potential loss incurred by the underperformance of the underlying share is totally offset (below the strike level) by the payoff of the put. The payoff of a long protective put strategy is paid at T, and is as follows:

$$Payoff_{Long\,ProtectivePut} = Max\{0, K - S_T\} + S_T$$

Basically, the portfolio manager is protected against downside movements below the strike level and can benefit from the potential positive performance of the underlying stock price. A protective put strategy has a cost equal to the premium the portfolio manager needs to pay to gain this extra protection, and this premium obviously depends on the moneyness and maturity of the put option. The shorter the maturity and the more out-of-the-money the put, the cheaper the premium. The profit formula from holding a long protective put portfolio could be written as follows:

$$\operatorname{Profit}_{Long\,ProtectivePut} = Max\{0, K - S_T\} + S_T - S_0 - Premium_{Put}$$

or

$$\operatorname{Profit}_{Long\,ProtectivePut} = \begin{cases} S_T - S_0 - Premium_{Put} & \text{if } S_T > K \\ K - S_0 - Premium_{Put} & S_T \leq K \end{cases}$$

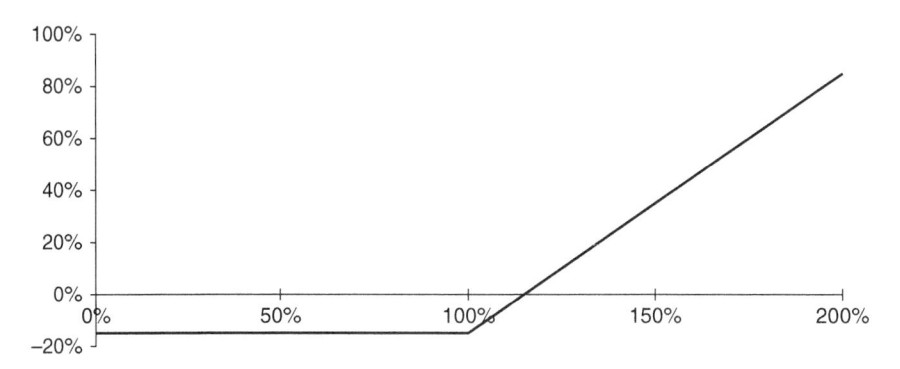

Figure 6.2 Profit graph associated with a protective put strategy

Figure 6.2 shows the profit graph from a long protective put strategy having been adopted. The strike is at-the-money, which makes the profit formula as follows:

$$\operatorname{Pr}ofit_{LongProtectivePut} = \begin{cases} S_T - S_0 - Premium_{Put} \\ -Premium_{Put} \end{cases} \text{if} \begin{array}{c} S_T > S_0 \\ S_T \leq S_0 \end{array}$$

This strategy is very different from a short covered call strategy, in that a long protective put position is a true hedge against significant downside movements in the stock price. Consider some scenarios assuming the market has decreased. When the put is in-the-money, the maximum loss that can be suffered from a protective put strategy is equal to $Premium_{Put} - (K - S_0)$. Since the put's premium is equal to its intrinsic value (here $K - S_0$) plus the time value, then the maximum loss when the put is ITM is equal to its time value. Now when the put used in the strategy is out-of-the-money, the maximum loss is locked at $Premium_{Put} + S_0 - K$, which is equivalent to the time value plus the decrease in the stock price up to the strike level.

Buying an out-of-the-money put would seem to be a good strategy. Indeed, the premium is lower, and the maximum loss is controlled. It is true that the probability of getting a positive payoff is lower than that of an in-the-money put; however, if the decrease in market price scenario is realized, the holder of the put benefits much more from the leverage properties of the option.

It is interesting to note that following a long protective put strategy is in a way equivalent to buying a call option. This could be verified by looking at the put/call parity, discussed in Chapter 4. Also, as shown in the profit graph in Figure 6.2, the profit of the protective put strategy, computed at maturity date, is the same as that of a long at-the-money call position, with a premium equal to the premium of the put (15% in the example).

The protective put strategy is particularly adopted by investors who wish to protect their bought equity assets immediately against any downside movement. The paid premium constitutes the insurance cost for the protection. It could also be followed by investors who have a portfolio that has already appreciated in value, and wish to protect against any downside market move during a particular period. They can choose to sell their stocks and realize their gains, but this could incur significant trading fees. Buying a put enables investors to avoid these high transaction costs and at the same time gain protection during the life of the put.

6.2 Vertical Spreads

By combining different vanilla equity options, an investor can play several market price scenarios. The vertical spreads are strategies that combine long and short positions in two options of the same type (only calls or only puts), written on the same underlying stock, and with the same maturity but different strikes.

Bull Call Spread

A bull call spread is a strategy where the trader buys a call with maturity T and strike K_1 and simultaneously sells another call on the same underlying with maturity T and strike K_2. In a bullish call spread strategy, K_2 is higher than K_1.

The payoff at maturity of a bull call spread strategy is as follows:

$$Payoff_{BullCallSpread} = Max\{0, S_T - K_1\} - Max\{0, S_T - K_2\}$$

or, formulated differently:

$$Payoff_{BullCallSpread} = \begin{cases} K_2 - K_1 & S_T \geq K_2 \\ S_T - K_1 & \text{if } K_1 \leq S_T < K_2 \\ 0 & S_T < K_1 \end{cases}$$

Figure 6.3 shows the payoff vs. the profit of a bull call spread strategy (call spread). The strategy exhibited in Figure 6.3 is composed of a long position in an at-the-money European call with a one-year maturity and a short position in a one-year European call with strike at 120%. The premium of the bought call is equal to 15% in the example, and the premium of the sold call option is equal to 8%. This means that the price to acquire the call spread is equal to 15% − 8% = 7%. The profit at maturity is equal to the payoff minus the call spread premium. The maximum payoff is capped at the difference between both strikes, i.e. 120% − 100% = 20%. That makes the maximum profit from this strategy equal to 20% − 7% = 13%.

The call spread strategy could be used as a limited hedge or to speculate on the price behavior at maturity of a specific underlying stock. Here, the term "limited hedge" is used deliberately, as the hedging benefit from a call spread is only valid up to the higher strike price level. One might also speculate on a slight increase of a particular stock's price and would then buy a call spread to gain benefit from this scenario using a cheaper derivative. Indeed, the premium of a call option might be quite expensive; a call spread would be a great alternative (cheaper premium) for the cases where the investor expects increases in the underlying's price up to a particular level (usually the higher strike price).

Call spreads are also widely used by traders to hedge other offered options such as digital options. A bullish cash-or-nothing digital option is one that pays the holder a pre-determined fixed cash amount if the underlying's stock price at maturity ends up higher than the pre-determined strike price. The prices of digital options are usually derived from the call spreads used to replicate the payoff. Usually, the call spreads used

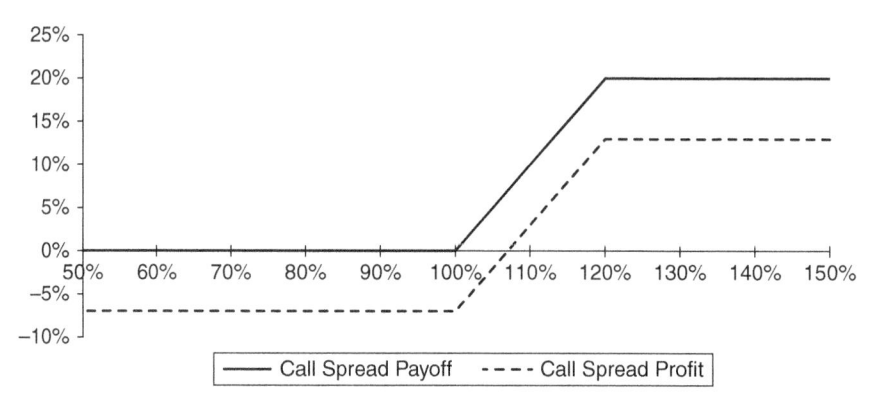

Figure 6.3 Payoff and profit of a call spread strategy

as a hedge have the upper strike price equal to the digital's strike price. This implies that the hedge payoff is always equal to or greater than the digital payoff; and the offered digital price is at least equal to the hedge cost (call spread price) – this is called an overhedge.

EXERCISE

Let's consider the case of Lamia Bouzoubaa, a fund manager who has a bullish view on a European share Stock Y. After discussion with an equity analyst following this particular share, she is now convinced that Stock Y is about to increase by around 10% in the next three months. She decides to buy a leveraged derivative instrument to help her take a profit from this scenario if it gets realized. She calls her brokers to ask for the premium of a three-month ATM European call on Stock Y as well as the price for a three-month call spread on the same stock with strikes at 100% and 110%. These are the prices she gets over the phone:

- three-month ATM call on Stock Y: Premium = 8%
- three-month call spread on Stock Y with strikes at 100% and 110%: Premium = 3%.

The prices above are expressed in percentage of notional terms. According to her expectations, Lamia decides to buy the call spread. Notional is equal to €5,000,000. At the maturity date, the stock price has increased by 7%.

Compute her P&L in euros, and explain why her decision was the best to take in her particular case.

Discussion

Why the choice to buy the call spread:
First, let's analyze Lamia's market view. She expects the underlying stock's price to increase by 10% after three months, and she wants the most efficient derivative that will help her profit the most from this view if it is realized. If that scenario proves true, the payoff from the ATM call option would be equal to €5,000,000 × 10% = €500,000. And the profit from a long call option strategy would be equal to the payoff minus the

premium, i.e. €5,000,000 × (10% − 8%) = €100,000. The call spread alternative would have given the same payoff but at a cheaper premium, which makes the expect profit from Lamia's perspective equal to €5,000,000 × (10% − 3%) = €3,500,000. This is why Lamia's expectations originally led her to choose to buy the call spread instead of the call option.

Profit and Loss from the call spread strategy:
After three months, the market price of Stock Y has increased by 7%, which falls between the two strikes of the call spread. The payoff from Lamia's strategy is equal to €5,000,000 × 7% = €3,500,000. The premium being equal to €5,000,000 × 3% = €1,500,000, the profit from the call spread strategy is equal to €2,000,000. If she had bought the call option, the profit would have been negative, as the 7% payoff would have been lower than the 10% premium.

6.3 Bear Put Spread

A bear put spread strategy is a strategy where the holder buys a put with maturity T and strike K_2 and simultaneously sells another call on the same underlying with maturity T and strike K_1. In a bearish put spread strategy, K_2 is higher than K_1.

The payoff at maturity of a bear put spread strategy could be written as follows:

$$Payoff_{BearPutSpread} = Max\{0, K_2 - S_T\} - Max\{0, K_1 - S_T\}$$

or, formulated differently:

$$Payoff_{BearPutSpread} = \begin{cases} K_2 - K_1 & S_T \leq K_1 \\ K_2 - S_T & \text{if } K_1 < S_T \leq K_2 \\ 0 & S_T > K_2 \end{cases}$$

Figure 6.4 shows the payoff at maturity (straight line) of a put spread strategy where the trader bought an at-the-money European put and sold an out-of-the-money European put with strike at 80% (again compared to the initial price of underlying stock). At the inception of the trade, the investor pays 16% premium for the bought ATM put and receives 9% on the trade notional as a premium for the sold OTM put option; so the premium paid here to adopt this bear put spread strategy is equal to 16% − 9% = 7%. The graphs in Figure 6.4 depend on the underlying's price at maturity (the x-axis).

The graphs in dotted line give a comparison between the profit from buying an ATM put and following a put spread strategy with strikes at 100% and 80%, depending on the price at expiry date of the underlying stock price. The payoff being equal to the payoff at maturity less the premium of the strategy, the figure shows which cases are more suitable for buying a put compared to a put spread with the same maturity date. When the market price at maturity is very low, it is worth better buying a put option. For smaller changes in the stock price, the profit from a put spread strategy is better, as the payoff would be the same compared to a European put with strike K_2 but the premium is much cheaper.

As is the case for call spreads, the put spread strategy could be used as a limited hedge or to speculate on the price behavior at maturity of a specific underlying stock.

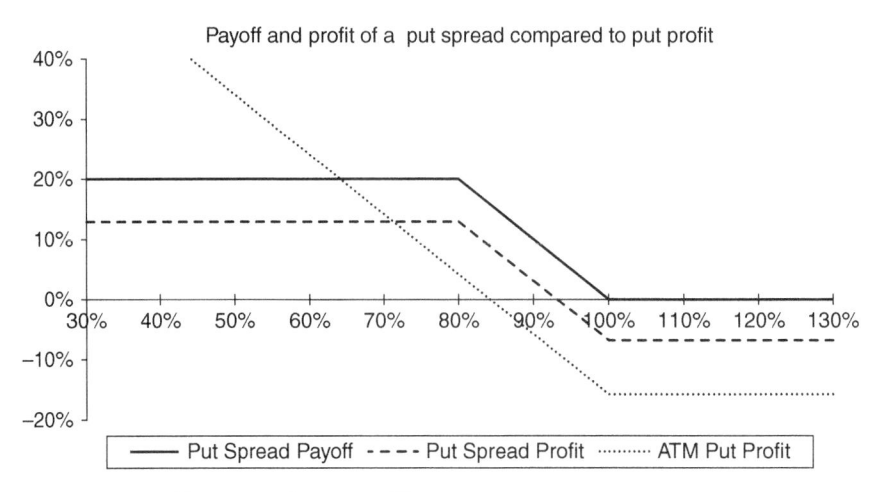

Figure 6.4 Bearish put spread versus vanilla put

Here, the term "limited hedge" is used deliberately, as the hedging benefit from a put spread is only valid for downside moves down to the lower strike price level. One might also speculate on a slight decrease of a particular stock's price and would then buy a put spread to get benefit from this scenario using a cheaper derivative. Indeed, the premium for a European put option might be quite expensive; a put spread would be a great alternative (lower premium) in the cases where the investor expects slight decreases in the underlying's price down to a particular level (usually the lower strike price K_1).

EXERCISE

Meriem Eulj is a successful trader that made significant profits in the past by following the stocks in the US energy sector. She believes the quarterly results of Stock Z that would be announced in two days will be much worse than expected by the market. Therefore, she anticipates a decrease of 10% of the price of Stock Z, in the month following the announcement of the results. Today, the premium for a one-month ATM European put on Stock Z is equal to 4.2%, and the price for a one-month put on the same underlying stock with strike at 85% is equal to 1.2%. For which underlying prices at maturity would the profit from the ATM put be greater than that of a one-month put spread on Stock Z with strikes at 100% and 85%?

Discussion

First, compute the put spread premium. It is equal to $4.2\% - 1.2\% = 3\%$. Then compute the price at maturity S_T under which the profit from the put is greater than that of the put spread. Here, the higher strike of the put spread (100%) is equal to the strike of the ATM put. Let's find S_T for which:

$$\text{Profit}_{Put} = \text{Profit}_{PutSpread}$$

then

$$Payoff_{Put} - 4.2\% = Payoff_{PutSpread} - 3\%$$
$$Max\{0, 100\% - S_T\} - 4.2\% = Max\{0, 100\% - S_T\} - Max\{0, 85\% - S_T\} - 3\%$$

After simplifying, we get

$$Max\{0, 85\% - S_T\} = 1.2\%$$

This equation could not be verified if $S_T > 85\%$. We only consider cases where the underlying's price at expiry date is lower than 85% of the initial spot price.

$$85\% - S_T = 1.2\%$$

Eventually $S_T = 83.8\%$

If Stock Z's price at maturity lies in the range [0%; 83.8%], the profit from buying the at-the-money put would be higher than that of the 100%/85% put spread.

The strategies presented above are called vertical spreads, as they consist of buying and selling options of the same type, with similar maturities and different strikes. Horizontal spreads are another type of spread that consist of simultaneously buying and selling options of the same type (calls or puts), written on the same underlying stock with the same strike but different maturities.

6.4 Collars and Three-Ways

A collar strategy is a method used by investors who already hold a portfolio of stocks and want to gain protection against adverse market moves. A collar strategy is a combination of the following positions:

- Long a particular stock.
- Short a risk-reversal strategy on the same stock, itself a combination of the following positions:
  - Long a European put with strike K_1 and maturity T.
  - Short a European call with strike K_2 and maturity T.

The payoff at T of a short risk-reversal is as follows:

$$Payoff_{ShortRiskReversal} = Max\{0, K_1 - S_T\} - Max\{0, S_T - K_2\} \text{ with } K_2 > K_1$$

or

$$Payoff_{ShortRiskReversal} = \begin{cases} K_1 - S_T & S_T \leq K_1 \\ 0 & \text{if } K_1 < S_T \leq K_2 \\ K_2 - S_T & S_T > K_2 \end{cases}$$

The risk-reversal position is usually done at zero-cost; that is, the strikes of the call and put options are chosen around S_0 such that the premium of the bought put is equal to the premium of the sold call.

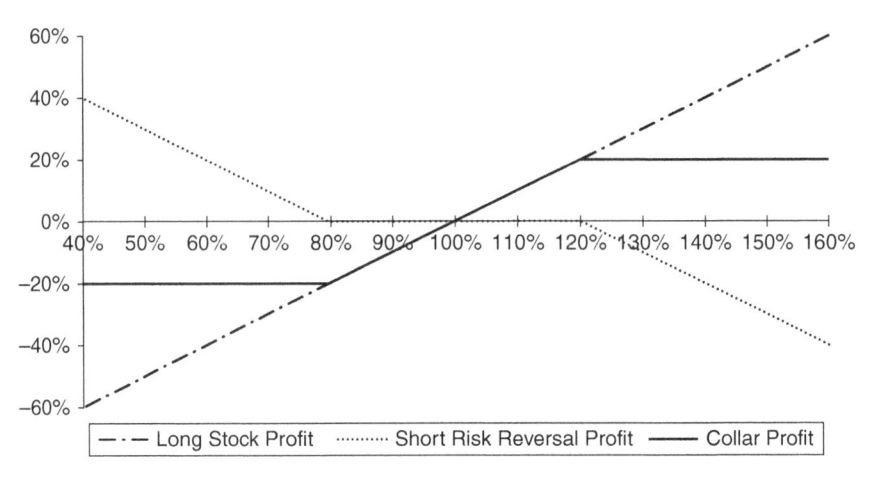

Figure 6.5 Profit at maturity from an equity collar composed of a long position in the underlying stock and a zero-cost short risk-reversal position with strikes at 80% and 120%.

It is very interesting to understand the similarities between a short forward position and a short risk-reversal position. A zero-cost short forward position enables an investor to lock the selling price at the pre-agreed strike K at maturity T. It is equivalent to a long European put and a short European call positions on the same underlying stock, with strike K and maturity T (ref put/call parity). Similarly, a short risk-reversal position is equivalent to a long put and short call positions written on the same underlying stock with maturity dates equal to T. However, the strikes K_1 and K_2 are different and oscillate around K in the case of a zero-cost short risk-reversal position. The premium received from the sold out-of-the-money call is used to buy the out-of-the-money put.

Figure 6.5 shows the total value at maturity T of a portfolio of stocks protected by a short risk-reversal strategy to create a collar strategy. Here the zero-cost risk-reversal is composed of a long put position with strike at 80% and a short call position with strike at 120%. The result is to lock the maximum loss at T to $100\% - 80\% = 20\%$ and the maximum gain at T to $120\% - 100\% = 20\%$. Compared to being short a forward, the maximum loss is capped using the put's strike. To pay for the put option, the investor sells a call option and cannot gain any advantage of an increase in the stock's price above the call's strike. However, any positive performance of the underlying's price up to the call's strike contributes to an increase in the portfolio's profit.

Now that we've seen that a hedge can be realized using forwards and risk-reversals, let's explore another not-so-different alternative. A three-way can be realized by buying a European put and selling a call spread (instead of a European call).

The payoff at T of a three-way is as follows:

$$Payoff_{3-way} = Max\{0, K_1 - S_T\} - Max\{0, S_T - K_2\} + Max\{0, S_T - K_3\}$$

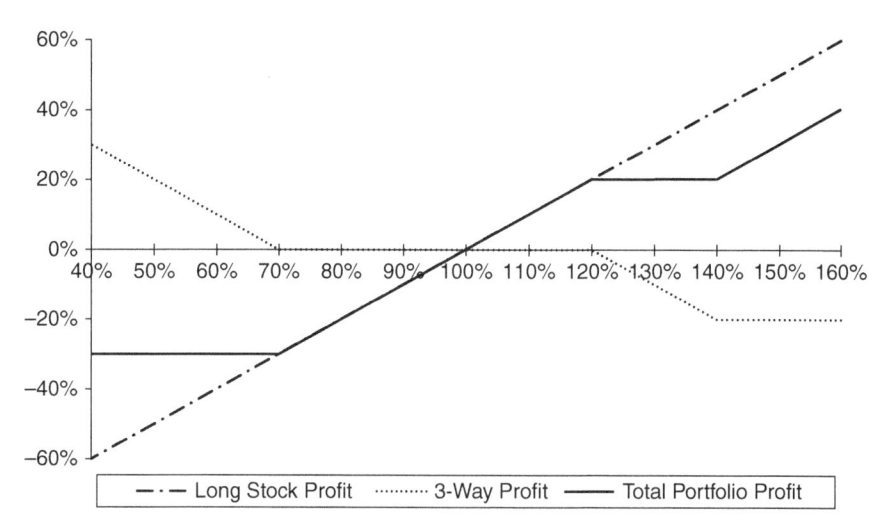

Figure 6.6 Profit at maturity from adding a three-way with strikes at 60%/80%/130% to a stock portfolio

Where $K_3 > K_2 > K_1$ or, written differently,

$$Payoff_{3-way} = \begin{cases} K_1 - S_T & S_T \leq K_1 \\ 0 & K_1 < S_T \leq K_2 \\ K_2 - S_T & K_2 < S_T \leq K_3 \\ K_2 - K_3 & S_T > K_3 \end{cases} \text{ if }$$

Figure 6.6 could be compared to Figure 6.5. Selling a call spread with strikes at 120% and 140% enables the investor to benefit from increases in the underlying stock price of between 100% and 120%, and also above 140%. Here, the premium received from the sold call spread is only sufficient to buy a put with strike at 70%. So the maximum loss is locked at 30% instead of 20%, as the investor gains protection when the stock price decreases below the put's strike, and suffers all the losses between 100% and 70% of the initial stock price.

Note that a three-way strategy could be performed at zero-cost, as shown in Figure 6.6. However and as is the case for risk-reversals and forwards, the strikes could be chosen at the client's convenience such that one of the counterparties should pay the fair price of the contract at the initial date.

6.5 Butterfly and Condor Spreads

When an investor uses vertical spreads, they consider the direction of the underlying stock's price (increase or decrease up to a specific level). Now we will see how combinations of vanilla options can be used to speculate on the volatility/stability of the underlying's price at maturity T.

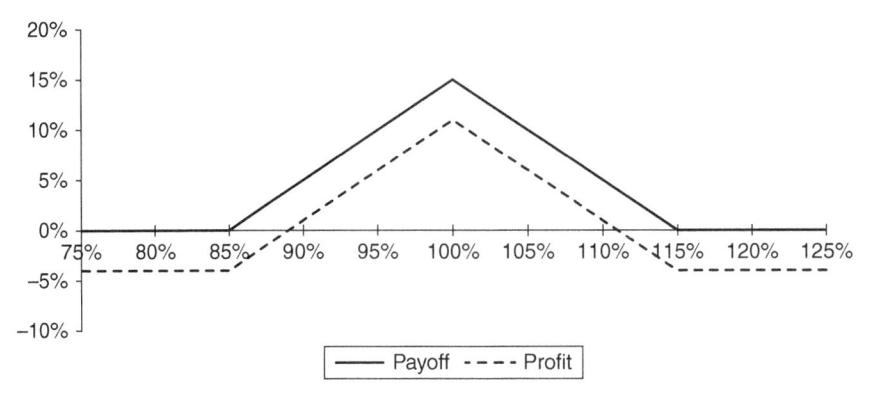

Figure 6.7 Payoff and profit of a short butterfly spread strategy

Butterfly Spread

A short butterfly spread can be realized using the following positions:

- Long a European call with strike K_1.
- Long a European call with strike K_2.
- Short 2 European calls with strike K.

All the options above are written on the same underlying stock and have the same maturity, T. Also note that $K = \frac{K_1 + K_2}{2}$

Figure 6.7 shows the payoff and profit at expiry date T of a short butterfly spread position where the following positions are combined:

- Long a European call with strike at 85% and premium of 12%.
- Long a European call with strike at 115% and premium of 4%.
- Short 2 European calls with strike at 100% and individual premium of 6%.

The premium paid by the short butterfly spread counterparty is equal to $12\% + 4\% - 2*6\% = 4\%$. The maximum payoff of a short butterfly spread strategy is equal to $K - K_1$; and this happens when the market price at maturity is equal to K. In this example, the maximum payoff for the short party is equal to $100\% - 85\% = 15\%$ and the maximum profit is locked at $15\% - 4\% = 11\%$. A short butterfly spread strategy could be used to speculate on the stability of a specific underlying stock's price around K at T. The counterparty long the butterfly spread has the opposite view and wishes to earn a maximum gain equal to the strategy's premium if there is a significant move in the stock's price.

Using the put/call parity detailed in Chapter 4, we can observe that it is possible to create the same short butterfly spread position using put options instead of calls:

- Long a European put with strike K_1.
- Long a European put with strike K_2.
- Short 2 European puts with strike K.

$$K = \frac{K_1 + K_2}{2}.$$

Replicating this strategy using puts instead of calls could be useful if the call options needed are either not available or liquid enough in the market. Executing a butterfly spread can be difficult, as it involves simultaneously negotiating and trading three different options.

Condor Spread

A short condor spread strategy can be realized using the following four positions:

- Long a European call with strike K_1.
- Long a European call with strike K_4.
- Short a European call with strike K_2.
- Short a European call with strike K_3.

Here $K_4 - K_3 = K_3 - K_2 = K_2 - K_1$ and $K_4 > K_3 > K_2 > K_1$.

All the options above are written on the same underlying stock, and have the same maturity, T. The payoff of a short condor spread position is as follows:

$$Payoff_{ShortCondorSpread} = \begin{cases} 0 & S_T \leq K_1 \\ S_T - K_1 & K_1 < S_T < K_2 \\ K_2 - K_1 & \text{if } K_2 \leq S_T < K_3 \\ K_4 - S_T & K_3 \leq S_T < K_4 \\ 0 & S_T \geq K_4 \end{cases}$$

Here again, the investor has a bearish view on the volatility of the underlying stock. They believe that the market price of the underlying stock will slightly increase or decrease at maturity T.

Figure 6.8 shows the payoff and profit at expiry date T of a short condor spread position where the following positions are combined:

- Long a European call with strike at 85% and premium of 12%.
- Long a European call with strike at 115% and premium of 4%.
- Short a European call with strike at 95% and premium of 8%.
- Short a European call with strike at 105% and premium of 5%.

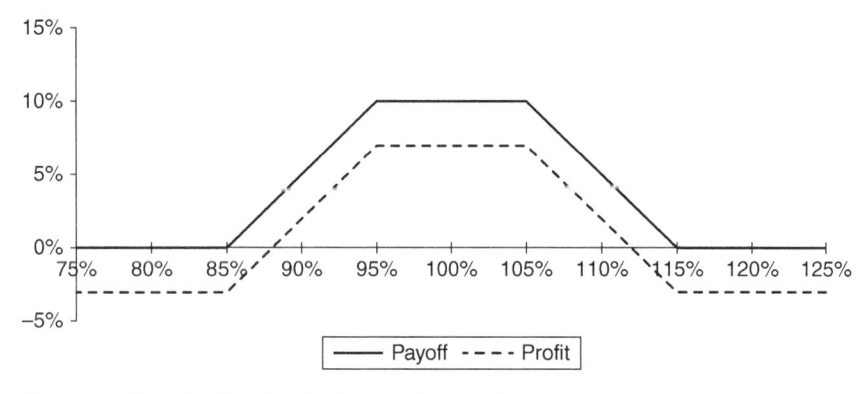

Figure 6.8 Payoff and profit of a short condor spread strategy

The premium paid by the short condor spread counterparty is equal to 12% + 4% − 8% − 5% = 3%. The maximum payoff of a short condor spread strategy is equal to $K_2 − K_1$; and this happens when the market price at maturity is between K_2 and K_3. In Figure 6.8, the maximum payoff for the short counterparty is equal to 95% − 85% = 10%, and the maximum profit is locked at 10% − 3% = 7%. A short condor spread strategy can be used to speculate on the stability of a specific underlying stock's price at maturity, at a cheaper price than a butterfly spread (and obviously a lower expected payoff). The counterparty long the butterfly spread takes the opposite view, and wishes to earn a maximum gain equal to the strategy's premium if the volatility increases more than expected.

As is the case for butterfly spreads, a short condor spread position could be taken using put options instead of calls:

- Long a European put with strike K_1.
- Long a European put with strike K_4.
- Short a European put with strike K_2.
- Short a European put with strike K_3.

with $K_4 − K_3 = K_3 − K_2 = K_2 − K_1$ and $K_4 > K_3 > K_2 > K_1$.

Note that the execution phase of a condor spread can prove to be tricky, as the trader needs to negotiate four different options at the same time.

6.6 Straddles and Strangles

Straddles and strangles differ from the spread strategies presented earlier in this chapter, in that they are composed of European options of a different nature (combining calls and puts). The maturities are, however, the same.

Straddles

A straddle is a derivative product where the buyer is long a European call and a European put with the same features; that is, the strike K, the maturity T and the underlying stock are all the same. The payoff at maturity of a straddle could be expressed as follows:

$$Payoff_{Straddle} = Max\{0, S_T − K\} + Max\{0, K − S_T\}$$

or

$$Payoff_{Straddle} = \begin{cases} S_T − K \\ K − S_T \end{cases} \text{if} \begin{matrix} S_T \geq K \\ S_T < K \end{matrix}$$

The payoff is always positive. In fact, the direction (up or down) of the change in the underlying's price is not important here. The most crucial factor is the amplitude of change, as the payoff of the straddle is equal to the absolute value of the underlying's performance. To be long a straddle, one needs to pay a premium at the inception of the trade equal to the call's price plus the put's price.

Figure 6.9 shows the payoff and profit at maturity of a long straddle strategy where the trader bought an at-the-money European put and an at-the-money European call.

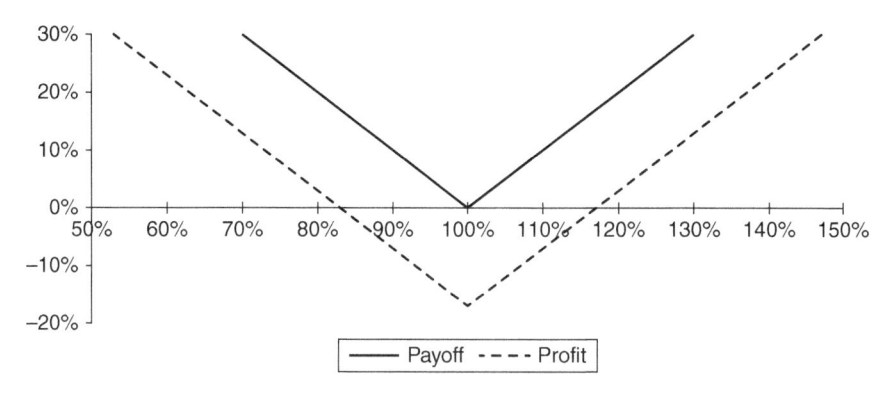

Figure 6.9 Payoff and profit of a long straddle strategy

The premium of the call is equal to 9% whereas the premium of the put is equal to 8%. The long investor pays a premium equal to 17% to buy this straddle. From this example, we can see that the payoff is very attractive as the investor can capture any change in price computed at date T. However, making a profit from this strategy implies that the absolute change in price should be at least higher than the premium of the straddles. Here, the underlying's price at maturity must have moved by at least 17% (positively or negatively) to result in a positive P&L.

Investing in a straddle is an almost purely volatility play where the long position believes the market price of the underlying security will change significantly from the initial date to the maturity date. This strategy is most often exploited by institutional clients that want to speculate on the underlying's volatility; a long straddle position corresponds to a bullish view on volatility. However, the premium needed to buy a straddle could be very high, so instead a long strangle position which has less payoff potential but is much cheaper can be followed.

Strangles

A strangle is also a combination of a European put and call, on the same underlying with the same maturity date. However, the strikes are different and chosen such that both options are usually out-of-the-money. The payoff at maturity of a strangle is as follows:

$$Payoff_{Strangle} = Max\{0, S_T - K_2\} + Max\{0, K_1 - S_T\}$$

with $K_2 > K_1$ or, expressed differently

$$Payoff_{Strangle} = \begin{cases} S_T - K_2 & S_T \geq K_2 \\ 0 & \text{if } K_1 \leq S_T < K_2 \\ K_1 - S_T & S_T < K_1 \end{cases}$$

In a strangle, the payoff is also always positive. In fact, the direction (up or down) of the change in the underlying's price is not important here. A strangle is much cheaper than a straddle, especially when both options are out-of-the-money.

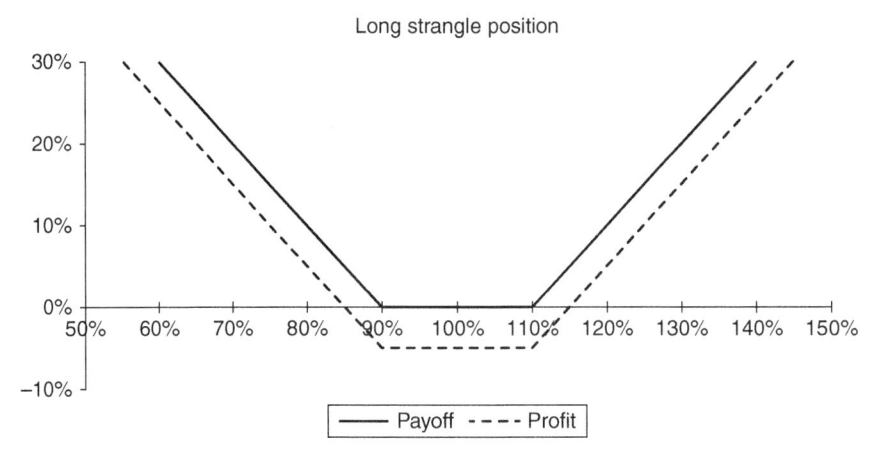

Figure 6.10 Payoff and profit of a long strangle strategy

Figure 6.10 emphasizes the payoff and profit at maturity of a long strangle strategy where the investor has simultaneously bought an OTM European put with strike at 90% and an OTM European call with strike at 120%. The premium of the call is equal to 3% whereas the premium of the put is equal to 2%. The long investor pays a premium equal to 5% to buy this straddle. The payoff is null if the absolute performance is less than 10%, and the profit becomes positive when the absolute performance calculated at T exceeds 15%.

Investing in a straddle is also an almost purely volatility trade when the long position has a bullish view on volatility. The short counterparty sells the strangle to earn a maximum amount equal to the premium, and expects the change in price not to exceed either of the two strikes.

7 Yield Enhancement Solutions

7.1 Equity Structured Notes

Equity structured notes became very popular at the end of the 1990s; they were issued by banks in response to their clients' investment needs. Equity notes are not usually used for hedging purposes. On the contrary, they are a response to a willingness to speculate on the behavior of a specific underlying asset during a particular period. The clients involved are hedge funds and institutions; and treasury managers of large corporations sometimes become interested in equity structured notes.

The capital at risk is most often 100% guaranteed; that is, the investor pays 100% of notional at trade inception to acquire the equity note, and receives a payoff of at least a guaranteed reimbursement of 100% of notional at maturity date plus a variable payoff derived from the price of an equity underlying security. This way, an equity note is quite similar to a bond, except that the coupons are neither fixed nor dependent on a market interest rate, but depend on an equity underlying asset.

The equity underlying could be a single stock, a basket of stocks or an equity index. The risk is controlled as the investor gets their money back at maturity. Their maximum loss is the risk-free rate they could have gained if they made a simple deposit instead. Equity notes have gained their popularity from the leverage effect incorporated in the variable payoff they offer. Fund managers like these financial products, as they enable them to have a guaranteed capital structure with a potentially high variable payoff. In some financial environments, interest rates are so low that investors prefer to risk this very limited risk-free rate to get a riskier but potentially larger payoff.

To make things clearer, here is an example of equity structured notes. At inception date, Investor A pays 100% of a notional of $10,000,000 to a bank, B (the note issuer). Assume the maturity of this note is three years. The payoff of this note occurs at maturity and is equal to:

$$\text{Payoff}_{\text{Note}} = \text{Notional} \times [100\% + 55\% \times \text{Max}\{0; \text{Perf}_{\text{S\&P}}(T)\}]$$

Where $\text{Perf}_{\text{S\&P}}(T)$ is the performance at maturity of the S&P 500 index measured with respect to the initial date. The minimum payoff is locked at 100%, and if the S&P 500 index increases by 40% in three years' time, then the payoff would be 100% + 0.55 × 40% = 122% of the notional. In our example, we assume a USD deposit rate in bank B of 5.5% per annum. A simple deposit for three years would have provided the investor with a gain of $(1 + 5.5\%)^3 - 1 = 17.42\%$.

In essence, an equity structured note is most often composed of a fixed-income part that guarantees full or part of the notional, and an option component that gives the

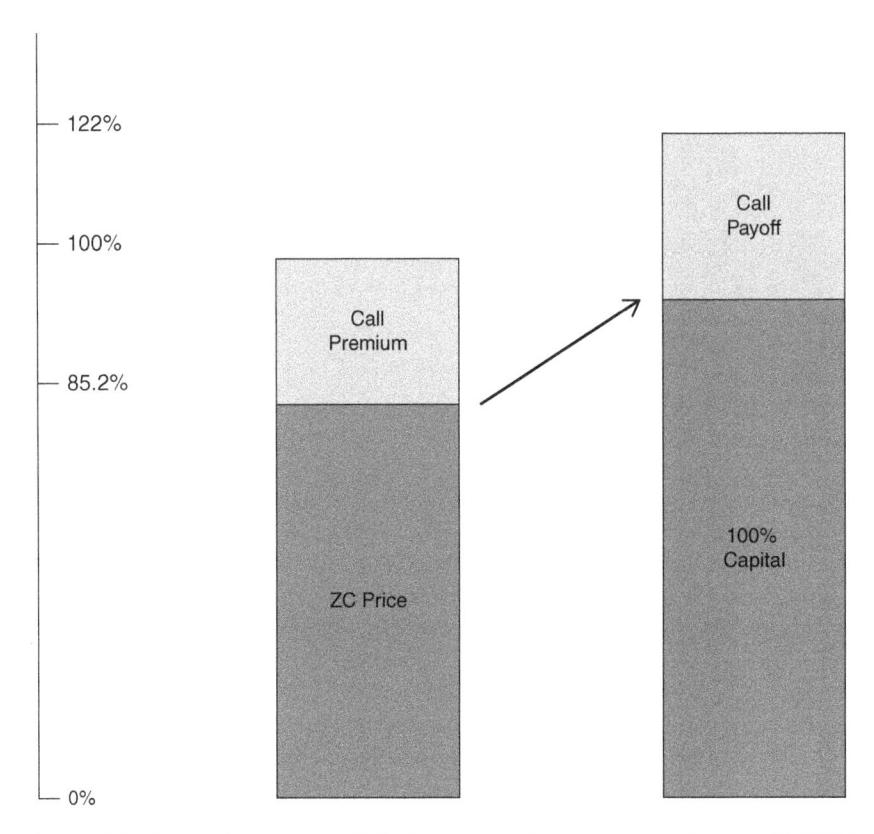

Figure 7.1 Composition and payoff of a three-year equity structure note based on S&P 500 index

holder a variable payoff based on a specific equity underlying. In our example, the fixed-income part is a zero-coupon bond issued by bank B. It is based on the risk-free rate as well as the CDS spread of the issuing counterparty. In our example, the USD risk-free rate is equal to 2% plus the 3.5% CDS spread of bank B. Indeed, the buyer of the note is exposed to the credit risk of the issuer only.

Figure 7.1 shows how the structured note in our example is initially priced, and how the payoff is determined at maturity. From the structurer's point of view, the structure of the note is defined according to the different market parameters on the initial date. To guarantee a payment at maturity equal to 100% of the invested capital, the structurer must price a three-year ZC bond paying 100% based on 5.5% interest rate. Its price is equal to $\frac{100\%}{(1+5.5\%)^3} = 85.2\%$. Now, the structurer still has $100\% - 85.2\% = 14.8\%$ to spend on the equity option part. Then they need to determine the participation on the European call written on the S&P 500 index. First, they evaluate the three-year call and find a theoretical price equal to 26%. If the participation is equal to 55%, then the theoretical price of the call becomes equal to $0.55\% \times 26\% = 14.3\%$. The sales in charge takes a 0.5% absolute sales fee charge on the notional, which makes the aggregate cost of the note's components equal to 85.2% + 14.3% + 0.5% = 100%.

It is important to understand that the guaranteed capital is only guaranteed *per se* by the issuer. Also, investing in a note does not mean that the investment is safe all the time up to the maturity date. The invested capital is locked during the entire life of the note. If the investor has liquidity issues and wishes to redeem their equity note at any point in time, the issuer has to provide them with a bid price – which could be lower than the 100% invested notional. Indeed, the price of the note at time t is equal to the price of the option part plus the price of the fixed-income component. And these values vary as the different market parameters fluctuate over time.

It is also interesting to note that the investor may be willing to take additional risk in order to get a potentially higher payoff. An equity structured note is OTC, and the payoff is adjusted to the needs of the client. If they wish, the guaranteed capital could be decreased (and may be lower than 100%) in order to permit investment in a more expensive (paying a higher expected payoff) option. The variable payoff derived from an equity underlying could be any option. The main idea is to get a safe part from the fixed-income product, plus a variable payoff that plays a particular market scenario.

Reverse convertible notes (reverse convertibles) are examples of structured notes with limited or no guaranteed capital. The reverse convertible note holder receives a payoff at maturity equal to:

$$\text{Payoff}(T) = \text{Notional} \times [100\% + \text{Coupon}\% + \text{Min}\{0\%; \text{Performance}(T)\}]$$

where Performance$(T) = S_T/K - 1$

The reverse convertible is composed of a long position in a zero-coupon note (paying 100% of the notional at maturity) and a short position in a European put option with maturity T and strike K. Coupon% corresponds to a fixed pre-agreed coupon that corresponds to the future value of the put's premium.

Basically, the reverse convertible note is suitable for an investor with a bullish view on a specific underlying stock. If the underlying stock's price expires above the strike price, the investor receives 100% of his capital plus a fixed coupon, which is the maximum payoff. Otherwise, the payoff is decreased by the absolute value of the negative performance of the underlying stock. This note is definitely not a capital-guaranteed note, as the potential paid payoff from the European put can exceed the received coupon at maturity.

In practice, reverse convertibles are structured such that the sold put is out-of-the-money, implying a lower probability of being exercised. Everything else being equal, the lower the strike price the lower the fixed coupon to be received at maturity.

7.2 Playing with Volatility

As we have seen throughout this book, the different market actors using equity derivatives are not only interested in the direction of the underlying's price; they could also be willing to play multiple scenarios based on different market parameters linked to the equity underlying itself. Many investors play the volatility of a particular share or stock index they are following. This could be useful in some specific cases. For instance, a company could be waiting for the decision on a very important trial or law that may significantly push the value of the share or index up or down. An investor with this information would be willing to use equity derivatives to get a long position in that share's volatility.

In fact, if an equity derivative has a non-zero vega, then it could be used to play a market scenario based on the volatility of the underlying. In the case of European options, one could realize a delta-neutral position to limit exposure on the spot price and have a unique position on volatility. Also, we have seen that it is possible to combine European options to create a product based on the volatility/stability of the underlying security. Straddles and strangles are bought if a stock's price is expected to make a large positive or negative move. Conversely, investors sell straddles and strangles when expecting the underlying stock price to remain stable.

Apart from combinations of vanilla options, there exist more complex derivatives that pay a payoff essentially based on volatility. Analysts sometimes agree that the price of a specific equity underlying could fluctuate within a particular range during a particular time period. Some options, like range accruals or wedding cake, optimize the profit if this scenario proves to be correct. For example, the payoff of a three-month wedding cake option could be as follows:

$$\text{Payoff}_{\text{Wedding Cake}} = \begin{cases} 6\% & \text{if } S_T \text{ expire within } [90\%;110\%] \\ 4\% & \text{if } S_T \text{ expires within } [80\%;90\%[\text{ or within }]110\%;120\%] \\ 2\% & \text{if } S_T \text{ expires within } [70\%;80\%[\text{ or within }]120\%;130\%] \\ 0\% & \text{otherwise} \end{cases}$$

If the price of the underlying stock expires at between 90% and 110% of the initial spot price, the payoff is maximal and equal to 6%. If the absolute performance is within [10%:20%], the payoff is equal to 4%. Now if the variation is higher and the absolute performance is within [20%:30%], the payoff decreases to 2%. This wedding cake option pays nothing if the price at expiry has changed by more than 30%. In this example of wedding cake, the option pays more if the price varies less. This option would be very useful for an investor that wishes to capitalize on the stability of the underlying stock; that is an investor who is short volatility.

A range accrual is an option that pays the holder a predetermined coupon times the percentage of days when the underlying's price stays within a particular range during a specific period. Here again, the payoff is maximal if the underlying stock's price remains stable within the specified range. The holder of a range accrual is usually short volatility inside the range and long volatility outside the range.

A very important thing to know about volatility is that the latter increases as stocks' prices decrease. Indeed, when a stock market crashes, it is accompanied by a very significant psychological impact on the different market players; fear and panic replace all the fundamentals of equity trading and the market becomes very emotional. Then the volatility of stocks increases very significantly. That is why investors with long positions in volatility through volatility derivatives are partially hedged against downside movements of stock markets.

When an investor adopts a delta-neutral strategy, path-dependency still exists, and the exposure to volatility is still not perfect. When market players are willing to get a pure volatility exposure, they traditionally invest in volatility swaps and variance swaps; these products offer the counterparties a position on the implied volatility and variance respectively. These financial instruments could serve as speculation and hedge vehicles. There are also some much more exotic derivatives based on the implied or realized variance, including corridor variance swaps, conditional variance swaps, and gamma swaps.

Eventually, investors could directly trade on derivatives written on volatility indices. These indices measure the implied volatility of specific stock indices. The VIX is one of the most quoted volatility indices; it is quoted on the CBOE and measures the implied volatility of the S&P 500 index. Other volatility indices exist for the most important stock indices. One cannot invest on the volatility index itself as it represents a formula only, but it is possible to invest in ETFs, futures and options written on these volatility indices. For example, an investor could buy a call option on the VIX if they believe that the implied volatility of the S&P 500 is going to increase during the life of the option.

And because of the negative correlation between a specific underlying's volatility and its price, many investors combine equity and volatility products. The VSTOXX is the index measuring the volatility of the Dow Jones EuroStoxx 50 index. Someone holding a portfolio of European shares could go long futures on the VSTOXX as a diversifying investment. If the price of the European shares drops, the VSTOXX would be expected to rise and the gain from the long futures position would compensate for the loss in the stock portfolio's value.

7.3 Equity Dispersion Derivatives

So far, we have explored equity derivates based on a single underlying. In the world of exotic products, however, many options and derivatives are based on a basket of stocks. We have seen how it is possible to trade on the price and/or volatility of a specific single stock or index, but it is also possible to trade on the way underlying stocks behave with respect to each other. The correlation between the underlying stocks then becomes a parameter of crucial importance. Options for which the payoff depends on how dispersed the underlyings are with respect to each other are referred to as dispersion options.

One of the most traditional dispersion derivatives are worst-of and best-of options. Assume these options are based on a basket of n stocks and let $S_1(t), S_2(t), \ldots, S_n(t)$ be the prices of these shares. Also, let $\text{Min}(S_T)$ and $\text{Max}(S_T)$ be the respective minimum and maximum values of $\{S_1(T), S_2(T), \ldots, S_n(T)\}$. The payoffs at maturity T of best-of and worst-of options with strike K are as follows:

$$\text{Payoff}_{\text{Worst of Call}} = \text{Max}\{0, \text{Min}(S_T) - K\}$$
$$\text{Payoff}_{\text{Worst of Put}} = \text{Max}\{0, K - \text{Min}(S_T)\}$$
$$\text{Payoff}_{\text{Best of Call}} = \text{Max}\{0, \text{Max}(S_T) - K\}$$
$$\text{Payoff}_{\text{Best of Put}} = \text{Max}\{0, K - \text{Max}(S_T)\}$$

The best-of call and worst-of put are respectively a call on the best performing stock and a put on the worst performing stock. Therefore, the payoff potential for best-of calls and worst-of puts are maximal. Their price can then be quite high. Conversely, the premiums of worst-of calls and best-of puts are much cheaper, but their expected payoff is much lower.

In the case of dispersion options, it is crucial to understand that correlation coupled with volatility play a role of great importance. For a worst-of put for example, the option's holder is long the volatility and short correlation, as this combination maximizes the payoff potential. The worst-of put buyer is said to be long the dispersion, as is the buyer of a best-of call.

Among popular dispersion options are outperformance options. They are commonly based on two underlyings, for which the market prices at time t are $S_1(t)$ and $S_2(t)$. Here again, the underlyings could be single stocks, baskets of stocks or indices. Outperformance options are typically European-style. At maturity date T, the payoff for the holder of an outperformance option is equal to:

$$\text{Payoff}_{\text{Outperformance}} = \text{Max}\left\{0, \frac{S_1(T)}{S_1(0)} - \frac{S_2(T)}{S_2(0)}\right\}$$

Basically, for an option based on the outperformance of S_1 versus S_2, the payoff increases if the performance of Share 1 increases above the performance of Share 2. For these options, the absolute performance is meaningless. Indeed, if both underlying stocks perform by 25%, the payoff of the option is still zero. The relative performance is the important factor. In other words, the greater the dispersion the greater the difference between both underlyings' performances, and the higher the outperformance option's price will be.

Investors interested in such options would like to gain a profit from a scenario where the performance of an underlying equity asset is compared to that of another asset. For instance, if an investor believes the European economy will increase much faster than the American economy in the next semester, he could buy a six-month outperformance option of the Eurostoxx 50 index vs the S&P 500 index. At maturity, if the performance of Eurostoxx index is equal to 18% and the performance of the S&P index is equal to 9%, then the investor receives a payoff of Max{0, 18% − 9%}= 9% of the specified notional.

In practice, most exotic options traders offering dispersion products are globally long volatility and short correlation, so they make money if volatility increases and correlation decreases. The vega position could be hedged; but it is much more difficult to hedge the exposure in correlation. When a market crash occurs, the volatility and the correlation increase as all stocks decrease significantly in value. And since the correlation exposure cannot be hedged, exotic traders can suffer significant losses during periods where the market is very nervous.

7.4 Dynamic Indices

Institutional investors usually search for products that create more wealth by using wealth. They can analyze the different sides of a market and decide to get exposed to this market. This could happen through investing in delta-one products or derivates based on a specific stock index. This is called getting a beta-exposure, that is, having a portfolio that moves the same way as the main market index. Now investors are willing to create alpha, an additional return on top of the market return.

The level of alpha desired depends on the investor's risk aversion. A higher expected return is associated with a higher level of risk, usually measured by the volatility. Ratios measuring risk-adjusted returns are often used to get an idea of how interesting an investment could be. Hedge funds are the usual suspects when it comes to generating alpha; hedge fund managers justify their ability to outperform the market by investing in their areas of expertise.

The problem that most investors face when it comes to putting money into hedge funds is a credit issue. Hedge funds have traditionally resembled black boxes; they lack transparency, and their strategies are most of the time discretionary. Many investors only understood their money was not in safe hands when they needed to redeem their funds. In some situations, the periodic valuations the clients were receiving were incorrect. And Ponzi schemes were discovered and publicized.

During the 2008 financial crisis, many investors lost large amounts of money. At the time of writing several years later, they are continuing to seek alpha, but they would like to have risk-control mechanisms and more transparency with regard to their investments. In response to this demand, banks have created dynamic indices; in addition to the diversification benefits of a traditional index, the risk of dynamic indices is somehow controlled or limited. The underlying assets composing the dynamic index are carefully chosen at inception. Then depending on the market behavior, the weights of the different underlying components are frequently or periodically rebalanced according to preset rules. Dynamic indices are so named as the weights are not constant but are continually rebalanced according to market movements, to maximize their performance.

The idea behind dynamic indices is to maximize the risk-adjusted ratios. The trading strategy is a predetermined algorithm. This way, the trading techniques and rebalancing decisions are known in advance. The transparency with respect to the trading strategy is maximized, and the assets chosen are usually stocks expected to increase in value. The rebalancing rules are mostly determined by back-testing. Objectives and constraints are initially fixed. Basically, depending on measures and ratios, if a stock's price is expected to increase in value, its weight is increased and the opposite happens when a stock's price is expected to drop.

The volatility of the dynamic index is usually fixed and set as a constraint. The objective of the dynamic index is to find a rebalancing rule that will maximize the return for the set level of volatility. There are also other marketed dynamic indices that minimize the volatility for a set level of return. This comes back to maximizing the risk-adjusted return. However, it is very important to keep in mind that this optimization process is based on back-testing, and of course past performance is not indicative of future results.

Many banks offer derivatives on their dynamic indices. Investors can even buy capital-guaranteed structured equity notes with a participation on the positive performance of an issued dynamic index.

Index

alpha, 94–5
American options, 49–52
Argentine crisis, 3
Asian options, 52–3
at-the-money (ATM) spot, 39, 40

banks
 risk management office, 18–19
 sales teams, 14–16
 structuring teams, 16–18
bear put spread, 79–81
best-of options, 93–4
beta-exposure, 94
binomial option models, 50, 71
Black-Scholes formula, 45–6, 55, 62, 64, 68
Black-Scholes-Merton formula, 45
Bloomberg, 10
borrowing, 8–10
bull call spreads, 77–9
butterfly spreads, 83–5

call loan, 9
call options
 see also options
 American, 49–52
 Asian, 42–3
 covered, 73–5
 European. see European options
call spreads, 77–9
cliquets, 68
collars, 81–3
commission fees, 15
condor spreads, 85–6
confirmation letters, 15
corporate clients, 19–20
credit rating agencies, 3
credit ratings, 3
credit risk, 3, 15, 29, 33
credit spread risk, 3

debt instruments, 4
default risk, 3
delta, 54–60, 69–70
 hedging, 59–60
derivatives, 6
 see also specific types
 delta of, 54–5
 dividend swaps, 35–7
 equity. see equity derivatives
 equity dispersion, 93–4
 equity swaps, 29–35
 playing with volatility and, 91–3
 pricing vanilla, 45–9
dispersion options, 93–4
dividends, 6–7, 35
dividend swaps, 35–7
down-grade risk, 3
downward-sloping yield curves, 4, 5
dynamic hedges, 44, 56, 59
dynamic indices, 94–5

equity derivatives, 6
 buy side of, 19–21
 delta of, 54–5
 risk control mechanisms, 18–19
 selling side of, 14–19
 structuring of, 16–18
equity dispersion derivatives, 93–4
equity forwards, 26–9
equity futures, 25, 28
equity structured notes, 89–91
equity swaps, 29–35
 applications of, 32–4
 benefits of, 32–4
 hedging, 34–5
European options, 39–43
 delta of, 55–9
 gamma of, 60–1
 pricing, 45–9
 relationships between Greeks of, 68–71
 rho of, 66–7

European options (*cont.*)
  straddles, 86–7
  strangles, 87–8
  theta of, 64–5
  vega of, 62
exchange-traded markets, 1

financial crisis (2008), 95
financial industry, regulation of, 15, 19
financial institutions, 19
  see also banks
float-weighted index, 2
following a short covered call strategy, 73–5
forward contracts, 26–9
futures markets, 22–5
  forwards compared with, 28–9
future value (FV), 6

gamma, 60–1, 69
government bonds, 3
Greek debt crisis, 3
Greeks
  choosing right model for, 71–2
  closed relationships, 68–71
  delta, 54–60, 69–70
  gamma, 60–1, 69–70
  rho, 66–8
  theta, 69–70
  vanna, 68
  vega, 61–3
  volga, 68

haircut, 32–3
hedge funds, 24, 95
hedgers, 24
hedging, 19–21, 27
  covered calls, 73–5
  delta, 59–60
  dynamic, 44, 56, 59
  equity swaps, 34–5
  limited hedges, 80
  protective puts, 75–7
  static, 44, 56, 59
  traditional, 73–7
hedging cost principle, 17, 43–5
historical volatility, 10–11
humped yield curves, 5

implied volatility, 11–12
index futures, 22, 25

indices, 1–2, 94–5
initial public offerings (IPOs), 1
institutional investors, 21
interest rates, 2–7
interest rate swaps, 20
in-the-money (ITM) spot, 39
intrinsic value, of options, 47–8
inverted yield curves, 4
investment barriers, 32
investors
  corporate, 19–20
  institutional, 21
  retail, 20–1

leverage, 23
LIBOR, *see* London Interbank Offered Rate (LIBOR)
limited hedge, 80
liquidity, 1
listed markets, *see* exchange-traded markets
log-normal distribution, 45
London Interbank Offered Rate (LIBOR), 4, 29
long protective put strategy, 75–7

margin accounts, 24
margin calls, 24
marketing department, 14–15
market risk, 19, 21, 33
misselling, 16
money, time value of, 6
Monte Carlo simulations, 50, 53, 71–2

Napoleons, 68

options
  American, 49–52
  Asian, 52–3
  best-of, 93–4
  delta of, 55–9
  dispersion, 93–4
  European. *see* European options
  intrinsic value of, 47–8
  pricing vanilla, 45–9
  time value of money, 48
  wedding cake, 92
  worst-of, 93–4
outperformance options, 94
Overnight Investments, 20
over-the-counter (OTC) markets, 1, 15–16

payoffs
  for American options, 51
  for Asian options, 52–3
  best-of options, 93
  for European options, 48
  expected, 71–2
  for options, 40–2
  for structured notes, 90
  for wedding cake options, 92
  worst-of options, 93
Ponzi schemes, 95
portfolio managers, 24–5, 66
portfolio risk, 19
present value (PV), 6
price/pricing
  futures, 25
  options, 39–40, 45–9, 50, 53
  spot, 25
  strike, 28
price risk, 19
price-weighted index, 2
propietary traders, 17, 24–5
protective puts, 75–7
put options
  see also options
  American, 49–52
  Asian, 52–3
  European, 39–43, 55–7, 60–1, 69–70
  protective, 75–7
put spreads, 79–81

regulations, 15, 19
relationship managers, 14
Repurchase Agreements, 20
retail investors, 20–1
Reuters, 10
reverse convertible notes, 91
reverse enquiries, 17–18
rho, 66–8
risk-adjusted returns, 95
risk control mechanisms, 18–19
risk-free rate, 3, 6, 66, 89
risk management tools, 54–72
  choosing right model for, 71–2
  delta, 54–60, 69–70
  gamma, 60–1, 69–70
  relationships between Greeks, 68–71
  rho, 66–8
  theta, 63–6, 69–70

vanna, 68
vega, 61–3
volga, 68
risk-reversal position, 81–2
Russian crisis, 3

sales fees, 15
sales teams, 14–18
Securities Lending Agreement, 9
short forward position, 82
short selling, 8–10, 25
skew, 12–13
speculators, 24–5
spot prices, 25
spreads
  bear put, 79–81
  bull call, 77–9
  butterfly, 83–5
  condor, 85–6
  vertical, 77–9
static hedges, 44, 56, 59
stock exchanges, 1
stock futures, 22–5
stock indices, 1–2
stock loans, 9–10
stock markets, 1–2
stocks, short selling, 8–10
straddles, 86–7
strangles, 87–8
strike price, 28
structuring teams, 16–18
swaps
  dividend, 35–7
  equity, 29–35

TED spread, 4
termsheets, 15–16
term structure of volatility, 12–13
theta, 63–6, 69–70
Three-month EURIBOR, 4
three-ways, 81–3
time value
  of money, 6
  of options, 48
total return equity swaps, 29–30
traders, 17–18, 66
trading, 17–18
Treasury bonds, 3
Treasury rate, 3, 4

upward-sloping yield curves, 4, 5

Value at Risk (VaR), 3, 19
value-weighted index, 2
vanilla options, pricing, 45–9
vanna, 68
vega, 61–3, 92
vertical spreads, 77–9
volatility, 10–13, 57, 62–3, 91–3, 95
   historical, 10–11
   implied, 11–12
   term structure of, 12–13
volga, 68

wedding cake options, 92
Whaley option models, 50
worst-of options, 93–4

yield curves, 4–6
yield enhancement solutions
   dynamic indices, 94–5
   equity dispersion derivatives, 93–4
   equity structured notes, 89–91
   playing with volatility, 91–3

zero-coupon notes, 91

Printed and bound by CPI Group (UK) Ltd, Croydon, CR0 4YY

Equity Derivatives Explained

Financial Engineering Explained

About the series

Financial Engineering Explained is a series of concise, practical guides to modern finance, focusing on key, technical areas of risk management and asset pricing. Written for practitioners, researchers and students, the series discusses a range of topics in a non-mathematical but highly intuitive way. Each self-contained volume is dedicated to a specific topic and offers a thorough introduction with all the necessary depth, but without too much technical ballast. Where applicable, theory is illustrated with real world examples, with special attention to the numerical implementation.

Series Editor:
Wim Schoutens, Department of Mathematics, Catholic University of Leuven.

Series Advisory Board:
Peter Carr, Executive Director, NYU Mathematical Finance; Global Head of Market Modeling, Morgan Stanley.
Ernst Eberlein, Department of Mathematical Stochastics, University of Freiburg.
Matthias Scherer, Chair of Mathematical Finance, Technische Universität München.

Titles in the series:
Equity Derivatives Explained, Mohamed Bouzoubaa

Forthcoming titles:
Smile Pricing Explained, Peter Austing
The Greeks and Hedging Explained, Peter Leoni
Interest Rates Explained Volume 1, Jörg Kienitz
Interest Rates Explained Volume 2, Jörg Kienitz
Dependence Modeling Explained, Matthias Scherer and Jan-Frederik Mai

Submissions: Wim Schoutens – wim@shoutens.be

Financial Engineering Explained series
Series Standing Order ISBN 978–1137–32733–8

You can receive future titles in this series as they are published by placing a standing order. Please contact your bookseller or, in case of difficulty, write to us at the address below with your name and address, the title of the series and the ISBN quoted above.

Customer Services Department, Macmillan Distribution Ltd, Houndmills, Basingstoke, Hampshire RG21 6XS, England